WITHDRAWN

THE LIBRARY OF THE WORLD'S MYTHS AND LEGENDS

Persian
Mythology

THE LIBRARY OF THE WORLD'S MYTHS AND LEGENDS

Persian Mythology

JOHN R HINNELLS

CHANCELLOR
PRESS

Half title page. Bull-head from column, the palace of Persepolis. (*See* page 93.)

Frontispiece. A gold plaque from the Oxus treasure showing a priest, magus, carrying the barsom – the sacred twigs associated with priesthood. This, rather than the kings of later Christian legend, is how the magi looked. The Oxus treasure, found by local peasants in 1877, appears to consist of votive offerings to a temple. It dates from Achaemenid times (sixth to fourth centuries B.C.).

Persian Mythology first published 1973

Revised edition published 1985 by Hamlyn

This edition published in 1997 by Chancellor Press, an imprint of Reed International Books Limited
Michelin House, 81 Fulham Road
London, SW3 6RB

Copyright © John R. Hinnells 1973, 1985

ISBN 0 7537 0000 X

Printed in Hong Kong

Dedication
To my parents.
'I can no other answer make but thanks,
And thanks, and ever thanks.'
Shakespeare

Contents

Introduction

Persia is a land of great contrasts: a land of deserts and jungle, of snowy mountains and luxuriant valleys; a place where apples and date palms grow within miles of each other; a land of oil wells and nomads.

Three mountain ranges form a triangle around the land – mountains which rise to a height of 18,000 feet (5,486 metres). At the heart of Persia lie two vast salt deserts. Within the mountain ranges are valleys, some as much as sixty miles (97 kilometres) long and twelve miles (19 kilometres) wide, with a climate like that of the Mediterranean countries. To the north, bordering the Caspian sea, lies dense tropical jungle. Rainfall varies from sixty inches (152 centimetres) a year in some parts to none in others. Although Persia has vast natural resources, it is only in recent times that they have been exploited, and apart from the famed 'Persian market place', agriculture is the traditional occupation.

Geography inevitably affects culture, and it is not surprising that in Persia there are a number of different cultures – cultures which in their turn have produced different mythologies. People in western Persia have always been open to influence from such centres as Greece and Rome, whereas those in the east have been influenced more by India and the Orient. Persia forms both a historical and a geographical bridge between East and West.

Our subject is that rich mine of poetry, folklore and myth which constituted much of the faith of ancient Persia. After a brief look at the history of Persia, the nature of our sources and the character of myth, we shall turn first to the ancient picture of the universe, the 'pagan' myths and the stories of the godly heroes fighting horrific dragons. Then we shall look at the highly ethical teaching of Zoroastrianism with its profound interpretation of traditional mythology. Once the national faith of Persia, Zoroastrianism is still devoutly practised by small communities in Persia (now part of Iran), and also by the Parsis in India, in the East and in the West.

Persia has been the home of a number of religious traditions. We shall examine the mythology of two of them: Zurvanism and Mithraism. Finally we shall consider the part mythology has played in the ritual, history and court of the land of the shahs. Most important of all, we shall try to understand the place of myth in the personal faith of the believer. This book, then, is concerned with both ancient and modern times, with history and with a living faith, albeit a small and sadly decreasing one. Space will not, unfortunately, permit us to examine all the different faiths which have moved into Persia, such as the Mandeans, Manicheans or Muslims.

Outline of Persian History

No nation's religion or mythology can be understood in isolation from its historical setting; some knowledge is needed of the cultural develop-

The Zagros mountains to the west of Persia. These and other mountains to the north and east formed a triangular barrier around the country which made invasion by foreigners, such as the Romans, very difficult.

ments and the various influences that were at work. Thus we must turn first to the history of Persia.

In the distant past the peoples now inhabiting Europe, Persia and India were all part of one group of tribes now referred to as the Indo-Europeans. Living perhaps in Central Europe, they gradually splintered off to form nations of their own. The Aryans, part of this complex of peoples, travelled south east, and in the second and first millenia B.C. invaded India and Persia. We must not imagine one vast organised army, but rather small tribal groups settling down independently until, after centuries, they became so numerous that they dominated the land.

The peoples who settled in India and Persia are known as the Indo-Iranians. Their religion is preserved in the collection of ancient Hindu hymns, the *Rig Veda*, and the ancient Persian hymns, the *Yashts*. Their religion reflected their way of life as nomads and warriors. They delighted in the beauty of nature, yet stood in fear of its venom and apparent malice; hymns dwell on the beauty of the dawn, and the terror of the drought. Their gods are either personifications of such ideals as Truth, or of natural phenomena such as the storm, or they are swash-buckling heroes who destroy the monsters which threaten men, Indra and Keresaspa for example (see p. 40).

Although both India and Persia have adapted and developed their beliefs far beyond this heritage, it is remarkable how much it still dominates their myth and ritual. Because the settlement of the Indo-Iranians was such a gradual affair, and archaeological remains are naturally so few, it is difficult to date with any precision their conquest of the land; however, by 800 B.C. they appear to have been dominant.

Zoroaster (the name is the Greek form of the Persian Zarathushtra) was the great prophet of Persia. Western scholars have until recently dated his life as 628-551 B.C., but further research suggests that he lived much earlier, somewhere between 1400 and 1200 B.C. This is important because it makes him the first of the prophets of the world's major religions, older than Moses, Buddha or Confucius. It is generally agreed that he lived on the Central Asian steppes north and east of Persia.

His teachings have come down to us in the form of seventeen hymns known as the *Gathas*. These are very difficult to translate because they are the only known examples of the language. As hymns they were produced to evoke known ideas to believers – to inspire, rather than to explain, beliefs to outsiders. There is a great diversity of scholarly opinion regarding the details of Zoroaster's teaching – especially with regard to the myths he believed in. As a trained priest Zoroaster was heir to a rich tradition; as a creative religious genius he reformed much of what he inherited. Rather like modern preachers Zoroaster tended to allude to the story of a myth and, without elaborating on it, drew out what he considered to be the significant moral or personal lesson, so that the myth might be made meaningful to his followers. What hints there are in the *Gathas* show that there was a substantial degree of continuity between his predecessors, the prophet and the later Zoroastrian tradition.

Zoroaster's originality lay not in the creation of new myths, but in the

This motif appears at the palace of Persepolis and thereafter in most forms of Zoroastrian Persian art down to the present day. The wings and central ring were based on Egyptian and Mesopotamian prototypes. Western scholars have usually interpreted this as a symbol of Ahura Mazda holding the ring of cosmic sovereignty with his hand raised in the traditional gesture of blessing. Parsis and some recent scholars doubt if this symbolises God himself, but rather the divine grace men seek and, on royal reliefs, the glory and power particularly associated with the divinely appointed monarch.

Opposite A winged figure from a doorway at Cyrus' palace at Pasargadae. It has been suggested that this depicts Cyrus himself, but it is more likely that it represents a protective spirit or genius of the royal palace. The crown is similar to that associated with apotropaic figures in the ancient Near East.

Right, top A lion's head from the top of a column at Persepolis. The lion is a traditional symbol of power.

Right, bottom A griffin's head from one of the columns at Persepolis. A number of motifs at Persepolis appear to have been taken from Babylonian art. It may be that some of the underlying ideology associated with royalty and cosmic powers was also incorporated into Persian traditions.

Opposite A bull's head which decorated the top of a column in the great hall at Persepolis (*in situ*). The bull is a widespread symbol of vitality and fertility.

interpretation he placed on old ones. Perhaps what characterised his teaching more than anything else was the emphasis on the personal side of religion. He believed he had seen Lord Mazda in visions, that he had been called and set apart from the beginning for his mission. All men, he taught, must choose for themselves between the forces of good and evil. Ahura Mazda, he preached, was wholly good. Everything in life which is evil emanates from Mazda's opposing spirit, his twin power in the universe, Angra Mainyu, the Destructive Spirit. Life in this world is caught up in the cosmic battle between them. Mankind has free will to choose between them, but by supporting good men will hasten the time when, on the day of judgment, with the aid of the saviours to come, evil will be overthrown and good will triumph. Then Mazda's rule will be established throughout creation. Individual choice, individual commitment, personal responsibility and personal judgment are the keynotes of the prophet's teaching. Because of the enormous difficulty of reconstructing the myths behind the dynamic but elusive poetry of Zoroaster's hymns, it was decided that in this book the Zoroastrian myths would be related from the later texts because, on the whole, they are more clear and full, but as the exposition proceeds it will become clear how faithful the later writers were to the preaching of their prophet.

Right The tomb of Cyrus the Great (near the palace at Pasargadae) is raised above the plain and visible from a great distance. Probably the setting was originally laid out as a royal park (paradise). Greek and Roman authors comment on the gold couch, table, vessels and coffin used within. Raiders (almost certainly non-Persians) have robbed the founder of the Empire of these possessions. Some scholars have suggested that tomb burial shows Cyrus was not a Zoroastrian since his funeral evidently did not involve exposure to carrion-eating creatures (*see* pages 128ff), but because the corpse is lifted up and separated from the earth by the stone plinths it does in fact conform to Zoroastrian purity laws.

Opposite left The mighty Persian king of kings is regularly depicted as larger than his fellow men to express the idea of his might. Here he is shown with attendants holding the royal emblems of fly whisk and umbrella over him and beneath the winged symbol (*see* page 9) on a relief depicting a procession at Persepolis.

Opposite, right Two views of a silver drachma showing Ardashir I the founder of the Sasanian empire. The fire altar on the reverse is somewhat like those of the exterior of the Achaemenid royal tombs at Naqsh-i Rustam (*see* pages 101–102) with its column and plinths, except this also shows claw-shaped feet.

The teaching of Zoroaster at first aroused great opposition, but when he succeeded in converting a local chieftain, Vishtaspa, Zoroastrianism began to spread. When it became the religion of the court of the King of Kings we do not know. The great Persian empire of the Achaemenids was founded by Cyrus the Great, who began as ruler of a small kingdom, Anshan, in south-west Persia. After invading Egypt and Lydia in Asia Minor and marching east into India, he turned his attention to the mighty empire of Babylon which, divided and demoralised, opened up its gates to the conqueror without offering any resistance. United for the first time, Persia was transformed by one man into one of the greatest empires the world has ever known. The policy of Cyrus and his successors towards the subject peoples was one of tolerance. They were given a remarkable degree of autonomy and were allowed to follow their own religions.

Although Cyrus was the founder of the Achaemenid empire, its great designer was Darius (521-486 B.C.). It may be that he was a usurper – we cannot be sure – but he was certainly a great military leader and administrator. A fervent disciple of truth and justice, he drew up a law code for the empire. As well as leaving for posterity the great palace at Persepolis, Darius has also left us many inscriptions which expound his understanding of his position as king. He refers constantly to the fact that it is by the grace of Ahura Mazda that he is king, and that it is he who gives success to Darius. All who oppose the king are of the 'Lie'. These inscriptions have been taken by many to show that by the time of Darius Zoroaster's teaching had permeated the empire and converted the King of Kings himself. Although the inscriptions make no reference to some of the central Zoroastrian teachings (to the Bounteous Immortals for example), they do suggest a religious belief similar to that of the great prophet. It is generally agreed that Zoroastrianism became the state religion of the Achaemenid empire, making it perhaps the most powerful religion of the then known world.

It was under Darius and his successor, Xerxes, that the famed invasions of Greece were attempted and the first 'marathon' was run. Towards the end of Xerxes' reign (d. 465 B.C.) Persia's military power began to decline, but it was not for another hundred years – until the rise of the mighty Alexander the Great – that she fell. The empire of the King of Kings was apparently drowned in the tide of Hellenism, yet Persia had no small influence on her conquerors.

In the third century B.C. the fight for independence began, and by 150 B.C. the Parthian empire emerged under Mithradates. The Parthians

Overleaf, bottom These winged creatures on the gateway of Persepolis are almost certainly taken from Babylonian ideas of supernatural beings who guard the entrances to religiously important places – such as a royal dwelling. If the Persians took over such art forms, did they also take over something of the concept of kingship (*see* page 99).

Above and above left Five Achaemenid kings had their tombs cut high in a rock face at Naqsh-i Rustam (4 miles or 6 km from Persepolis). This was an ancient Elamite sacred site. All the tombs followed the same pattern, one made by Darius (not the one on page 12). In the horizontal bar, palace-like doorways and columns were carved with the entrance to the tomb in the centre. Above this the king was shown standing on a platform carried on the shoulders of his subjects. With a bow in one hand, he raises the other in prayer (or blessing) and stands before a sacred fire burning on an altar. Behind the fire the sun and moon are carved. On the face of the reliefs royal inscriptions were carved in Old Persian (cuneiform). These tombs observe Zoroastrian purity laws by keeping the defiling corpse away from the good earth.

Opposite This series of coins illustrates something of the development in coinage from Achaemenid to Sasanian times. The first coin, a fifth-century Achaemenid gold daric, shows a warrior not unlike the archers at Susa. The second, an early Parthian silver drachma, is thought to show the head of king Mithradates I (c 171–138 B.C.). He is clean-shaven, following Hellenic fashion. The third coin is from the reign of Mithradates II (128–88 B.C.), showing the king bearded in Persian fashion. The reverse of the coin shows Arsaces, the deified ancestor of the Parthians. On the last two coins (a drachma of Shapur I, A.D. 241–272), and a gold denarius of Khusrau II, A.D. 590–628) the kings are shown wearing the ornate crowns of the Sasanian period. The modelling of the hair is similar in style to that on some of the Sasanian reliefs. Khusrau wears a crown with wings resembling the symbol for the god Verethraghna and the symbol of the moon god, Mah. He is also set against the background of the sun and moon, for the king is a cosmic figure. It is, then, not only the style but also the thought that has developed from the simplicity of the Achaemenid coin. American Numismatic Society.

different religious groups in the homeland itself: Zoroastrians, Zurvanites, Manicheans, Hindus, Buddhists, Greeks, Jews, Christians and pagans. The Christians in particular were a politically suspect group after the conversion of the ruler of Persia's greatest enemy, Constantine, to Christianity. Manicheism, a syncretistic cult, seemed to offer a possible solution to the problem, but largely as a result of the efforts of Kartir, a particularly vigorous defender of the Zoroastrian faith and a great power behind the throne, Zoroastrianism was confirmed as the state religion.

The political and economic history of Sasanian Persia resembles a swinging pendulum. In the fifth century Persia was torn internally by the rise of Mazdakism, an abortive form of communism, and in 484 the country was invaded from the east by the Ephthalites. In 531, Khusrau I, perhaps the country's greatest ruler, came to the throne. He defeated the Ephthalites and invaded Syria, but his greatest achievements were in the field of internal reform. He re-established the power of the monarchy, introduced fiscal, agricultural, social and military reform, the state control of education and a vast building programme. The stability which he achieved within the society was so great that it led eventually to the stagnation and decay of the state. The king himself was so revered by his people that the legend grew up that he had passed deathless into the hereafter and that he would return at the end of the world with an army to defeat the demons who would attack Persia.

In 610 Sasanian Persia gave to the world her swansong. Her armies swept westwards to the Bosphorus, Constantinople, Damascus, Jerusalem, Gaza and Egypt, all within the space of six years (610-616). But despite this outstanding military success, which gave Persia the appearance of a world-conquering power for centuries to come, she fell before the Islamic invasion in 651. Torn by internal strife, corrupt and divided, Persia could not withstand the

came from north-eastern Iran, not from Persia proper. In the early stages of their rule they made great use of Hellenic technical resources in their architecture, coinage and art, but as they gained experience and skill their national heritage emerged more and more clearly.

The Sasanians, with their base in Persia proper, overthrew the Parthians in A.D. 224. Under Shapur I (ruled c. 240–272) Persian armies invaded east through the Hindu Kush into India and the Kushan kingdom and westwards to Antioch in Syria and Cappadocia. There was an enormous problem in uniting such an empire, containing as it did so many passionate assault of the warrior missionaries of the world's latest faith.

The fall of the Sasanian empire meant the end of Zoroastrianism as a state religion. Under the successive empires of the Achaemenids, Parthians and Sasanians it had been, for some 1,200 years, perhaps the mightiest political force of the time dominating an area from north India to what is now Turkey. To its contemporaries, for example the early Christians, it must have appeared as *the* religious power of the day. But Zoroastrianism did not die *as a religion* with Muslim Arab invasion, it merely lost its political status. The Islamic conquest brought centuries of persecution, at times vigorous oppression, to Zoroastrians in Persia. Some Persians were, doubtless, attracted to the new religion by its vitality and doctrinal simplicity and converted out of conviction. Others capitulated under missionary and political force. Over the centuries the number of Zoroastrians dwindled until now when only some 17,000 are left in Persia (or Iran as it is again known). They are to be found mainly in the villages and towns of the desert, notably Yazd and Kerman. Perhaps what is remarkable is not that there are so few but that after 1,300 years of subjugation there are any. It is a tribute to the faithfulness and stalwart courage of his followers that the religion of Zoroaster is alive in the twentieth century. In this century their position has become somewhat more secure than before, though the rise of Islamic fundamentalism in the 1970s naturally raised the fears of many. Some emigrated West but, at the time of writing, so far the worst fears have not been justified.

But Persia is no longer the main centre of Zoroastrianism; that is now in India, especially Bombay. In the tenth century a small band of devoted Zoroastrians chose to leave their homeland rather than desert their religion and sought a new land of religious freedom. They settled on the north-west coast of India in the state of Gujarat. As the British developed the island city of Bombay in the seventeenth century, the Persians, or Parsis (people of Pars) migrated to India's commercial capital. There they began to acquire positions of real importance, dominating much of Bombay's trade, commerce, industry, politics and educational institutions. During the period of British rule in India only three Indians were ever elected to the English parliament. All three were Parsis. Parsis were also very active in the birth of the Indian National Congress. In the twentieth century they have suffered, however, from a common urban problem – a declining birth rate. This, combined with other problems such as emigration, has resulted in a dramatic decrease in Parsi population figures. They now total only 90,000, making them India's smallest racial minority.

From India Parsis migrated to other parts of the British Empire and trading areas, to East Africa, Hong Kong, Singapore, Australia and, of course, Britain. Since Indian Independence, and after political changes in East Africa, Iran and Pakistan, further emigrations have taken place to the North American continent. The result is that, although the number of Zoroastrians has shrunk, the religion is now more widespread around the world than it has ever been.

The Sources of the Myths

Our knowledge of the mythology of Persia is derived from a variety of sources. The most important of these is the Zoroastrian bible, the *Avesta*. Unfortunately, only that part of the *Avesta* which is used in the ritual has survived, approximately one quarter of the original. Although it was not written down in its final form until Sasanian times the contents are considerably older. Indeed, within the general Zoroastrian structure of the *Avesta* are reflected and preserved ancient, pre-Zoroastrian myths.

The most important part of this complex of material is the *Gathas*, the seventeen hymns of Zoroaster. Although they are exceedingly difficult to translate, the profundity of their teaching makes them rank among the most precious gems of the world's religious literature.

Above A Sasanian dish showing King Peroz, A.D. 459–484 (identified by his crown) hunting, a much favoured royal pastime in ancient Persia and a popular theme of royal art since it displayed the regal prowess. Freer Gallery of Art, Washington, D.C.

Opposite This head of an archer from the walls of the palace of Persepolis illustrates some of the characteristic features of Achaemenid art. Whereas Greek artists were fascinated by anatomy or the folds of robes across the body, the artists at Persepolis were more concerned with pattern, both in details, as here the curls of the hair and beard, and in general with the overall composition in the postures and dress of the figures.

The *Gathas* are embedded in the *Yasna*, a collection of prayers and invocations chanted during the Zoroastrian sacrifice of the same name. These texts are of diverse origins and date: one section, for example, is a pre-Zoroastrian hymn to the god Haoma (*Ys.* 9-11, see below p. 33), whereas others are evidently Zoroastrian compositions.

For the purpose of this book one of the most important sections of the *Avesta* is that which embodies the twenty-four *Yashts* or hymns to various gods. Although all these hymns are used in the Zoroastrian services many of them basically date back to the pre-Zoroastrian period. One hymn is *Yasht 10*, the hymn to Mithra; we will look at it later.

Other sections of the *Avesta* are concerned with ritual directions, more prayers and invocations. This whole collection of ritual material is preserved in a dead church language, Avestan, which few priests understand, but because the words are thought to have effective power it is important to them that they are preserved with absolute faithfulness. It is this reverence for the sacred word which has enabled the material to be preserved for so long.

The Pahlavi, or Middle Persian, literature embodies a great variety of types of material: expositions and defence of the faith, visionary and apocalyptic material, wisdom and epic literature, poetry and historical works. Many of them naturally reflect the thought of the age in which they were written, but some preserve the myths and beliefs of the *Avesta*. One text, for example the *Bundahishn*, is a collection of translations of Avestan texts on the act, nature and goal of creation. The work includes, of course, later scribal comment, and in using this book it will be important to try to syphon such material away, but long passages appear to reflect accurately the thought of ancient Persia. Large sections of another work, called the *Denkard*, simply summarise the contents of the *Avesta*. Within this one block of material, then, we have not only the theology, hopes and fears of the Zoroastrians faced with Muslim rule, but also the myths of pre-Zoroastrian Persia.

A number of Islamic historians showed an interest in the ancient history and beliefs of the conquered peoples, and we have a number of Islamic presentations of Persian mythology. The main one we shall refer to

in this book is the *Shah name*, an enormous work written by the poet, Firdausi. Firdausi turned a prose reconstruction of Persian history from the day of creation to the Islamic conquest into verse form. His source, now unfortunately lost, interpreted myths as historical narratives, so that many of the mythical gods or heroes appear as 'historical' kings or heroes. Although he suppresses most of those elements of the tradition which would be offensive to his Islamic readers, the author reproduces beautifully the spirit of the Zoroastrian texts. Much of the narrative retains a sense of the underlying significance of the cosmic battle between forces of good and evil, presenting it as an earthly battle between good kings and tyrants.

Turning further afield, we shall have to use the sacred texts of ancient India, the *Vedas*, particularly the collection of hymns known as the *Rig Veda*. These hymns were written down at a very late date but their content goes back to the period 1500-500 B.C. Although some allowance must be made for the influence of the indigenous beliefs, the *Vedas* appear to preserve many of the beliefs of the ancient Indo-Iranians and so they can

Right, top The throne room at the palace of Persepolis. This, naturally, is the pinnacle of the complex and was the goal of the annual tribute-bearing procession which seems to have been the primary function of this palace. The relief of the royal hero on page 103 is on the door jambs of this room.

Right, bottom 'Khusrau of the righteous soul' (or his father Kavad) shown on a silver bowl. In the upper scene he sits enthroned (in a style which influenced Byzantine art) among four courtiers and below he is shown hunting, a favourite Persian pastime. Hermitage Museum, Leningrad.

Opposite Buddhist fresco from the caves at Bamiyan in what is now Afghanistan but within the ancient Persian Empire. From the first to the seventh centuries A.D. Bamiyan was a Buddhist stronghold, although there was a great deal of Persian influence on the iconography.

be used, albeit cautiously, in reconstructing the faith of pre-Zoroastrian Persia.

These are the main sources we shall use, but there are many more: the inscriptions of the Persian Kings, the reports of classical and foreign authors, art, coins, reliefs and of course archaeology. But we must not expect too much from our various sources. Ritual texts, particularly hymns, whichever religion they belong to, rarely try to give a thorough explanation of a belief; they hint at or allude to teachings or myths the worshipper knows well. They move his heart rather than exercise his brain. The hymns we are using naturally make many allusions which we miss completely. Nor must we expect too much from the reports of classical and foreign authors: how accurate would a picture of Christianity be that was built up from the comments of outside observers? Evidence from art and coins is often ambiguous; if the same pictorial symbol can mean different things to different believers, how much more so to scholars from a different culture centuries after it was executed! The reconstruction of myth is often, therefore, a matter of debate among scho-

This photograph, taken some time ago, gives a good impression of the magnificence and size of the palace at Persepolis. The gateway (page 14) can be seen on the right looking across the stairways and the hall of a hundred columns to the doorways of the throne room in the distance. Although craftsmen from many countries were employed on the site, which took many years to build (through the reigns of three monarchs, Darius to Artaxerxes), there is, nevertheless, a genuine artistic unity to the whole which formed an inspiring prototype for much later Persian art.

lars. In this book controversial points have been avoided or noted wherever possible, reserving further discussion of such problems for purely academic studies.

The Nature of Myth

Before we turn to the mythology of Persia we shall do well to pause and consider the actual nature of myth. In everyday language 'myth' has come to mean that which is fanciful or untrue, a usage encouraged by the *Oxford English Dictionary* which begins its definition with the words 'Purely fictitious narrative . . .' This approach is completely misleading. It assumes that myths should be viewed as quasi-factual stories which are either true or false. But precisely what is meant by 'true'? In Aesop's fable 'The Fox and the Grapes' it does not matter whether the narrative is factually accurate; it is the significance and meaning of the moral that is important. In some ways myths are rather similar. What is important is not the historical accuracy of the narratives, but what they mean to the believer. It is their function in religion which distinguishes myths from fables. In his religion man attempts to explain his understanding of himself, of his nature and his environment. Myths, containing, in narrative form, man's reflections on existence, are the standard forms in which he expresses this understanding. A creation myth is more important for its reflections on the nature of the world, man or God, than as a rival to Darwin's theories concerning evolution. A myth of the virgin birth of a prophet or saviour is not important as a historical account of the mother's love-life, but rather as an expression of the place of the prophet or saviour in the faith of the believer.

Not only are myths expressions of man's reflections on the basic meaning of life, they are also charters by which he lives, and they can act as the *rationale* of a society. The established pattern of society is given its ultimate authority through mythical concepts, whether they be the concepts of the divine right of kings in Stuart England, or the tri-partite pattern of society in Indo-Iranian belief. This taught that the gods created society with a three-fold structure: some men were created priests, others warriors and a third group were created productive workers, so that all men owed their station in life to the will of the gods. Myths can function equally as exhortations to a high moral code and provide men with models by which they fashion their own lives.

But myths are much more than mere narratives or symbolic accounts. Because they relate the activity of the supernatural they are held to release or re-activate that power as they are recited in the ritual. As Christians believe that by ritually re-enacting the Last Supper in the Communion service Christ is made present for the

believer, so people of other religions believe that by dramatising a myth of creation, or of (as in Persia) the final sacrifice to be offered by the saviour, that same power active at creation or at the end is made present for the faithful. Through myth and ritual the presence of the sacred is secured.

Myths, then, provide charters for ethical and religious conduct; they express and codify beliefs; they are sources of supernatural power. Thus in looking at Persian mythology we are not looking simply at bogus historical narratives, nor just at beautiful and ancient poetry (though myth is often that as well). We are looking at the basic Persian world view, its understanding of man, society and God.

If a myth is to be effective as a symbol then it must employ terms and imagery meaningful to its hearers. The other side of the coin is, of course, that the imagery will not be meaningful to those of another culture. The danger, therefore, in re-telling myths in their original form is that a foreigner may seize on those elements which appear bizarre and so miss the deeper insights which lie behind the symbols. The readers may, in other words, look at the symbol and not at what is symbolised. If books on mythology simply tell the stories, they fail to present the myths as they really are – as part of a whole and living tradition. The last part of this book will, therefore, leave behind the outer shell of myth and look at the kernel – myths as they relate to: Zoroastrian worship and politics, symbolism and ethics; to the whole society; indeed to the basic under-standing of man and the world in Persian mythology.

Ancient Persian Mythology

The Picture of the Universe

The ancient Persians thought of the world as round and flat, like a plate. The sky, to them, was not infinite space, but a hard substance, like rock crystal, which encompassed the world like a shell. In its original perfect state the earth was flat, with no valleys or mountains, and the sun, moon and constellations stood still over the earth at the noonday position. All was peaceful and harmonious. But this tranquil state was shattered by the entry of evil into the universe. It crashed in through the sky, plunged down into the waters and then burst up through the centre of the earth, causing the earth to shake and the mountains to grow. The chief mountain was Mount Alburz which took eight hundred years to grow. For two hundred years it grew to the star station; for two hundred it grew to the moon station; for two hundred it grew to the sun station; and for the final two hundred it grew to the utmost limit of the sky. The mountain thus spreads through the cosmos, while its base is attached to the sky where it encloses the world. The roots of this cosmic mountain spread under the earth, holding it together, and from these roots grow all the other mountains. In the middle of the earth stands Mount Tera, the peak of Alburz, and from there to heaven stretches the *Chinvat* bridge over which all souls must pass at death on their journey to heaven or hell. The Arezur ridge on the rim of Mount Alburz is the gateway to hell where the demons discourse.

It was not only the earth that was shaken by the entry of evil into the universe. The sun, moon and constel-

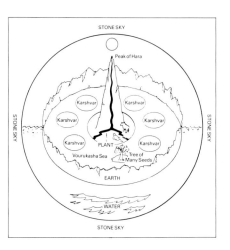

lations were shaken from their place so that they revolve round the earth like crowns until the renovation of the universe, entering the sky each day through one of the hundred and eighty apertures on Mount Alburz in the east, and setting through one of the hundred and eighty apertures in the west.

The rains were formed by the god Tishtrya (see pp. 25–7). They were blown together by the wind to form the cosmic ocean, Vourukasha, or boundless ocean, which lies beyond the peak of Mount Alburz. This ocean is so wide that it contains a thousand lakes, the springs of the goddess Anahita (see pp. 27–9). Within the ocean stand two trees: the Gaokerena tree, or White Hom, from which men will receive the elixir of immortality at the renovation of the universe, and the Tree of Many Seeds from which all other trees derive. In its branches lives the great Saena bird (later *Senmurw/Simurg*). When it beats its wings it breaks the branches, scattering the seeds which are then carried over the earth in the wind and the rain. Evil naturally tried to destroy this life-giving tree and

formed a lizard to attack it, but it is protected by ten *kar*, fish which swim ceaselessly round in such a way that one of them is always watching the lizard.

Then three great and twenty small seas were formed. Two rivers ran through the earth, one running from the north to the west and the other from the north to the east, both eventually running over the ends of the earth and mingling again with the cosmic ocean.

When the rains first came the earth split into seven pieces. The central portion, *Khwanirath*, forms one half of the total land mass and the surrounding six portions are referred to as the *keshvars*. Men were unable to pass from one region to another unless they rode on the back of the heavenly bull, Srishok (or Hadhayos). Srishok is carefully watched over by the righteous Gopatshah, half man and half ox, for he is to be the last animal to be offered in sacrifice at the renovation when all men are to be made immortal.

The bull is not the only remarkable creature in this ancient picture of the universe. An even more fantastic animal is the three-legged ass. Where it came from we do not know, nor do we know what the mythical beast was meant to be. One scholar has suggested that it was originally part of a meteorological myth since it is said to shake the waters of the cosmic ocean; others believe that it was originally a foreign god incorporated into

Persian belief. Whatever its origin, this holy animal is said to have three feet, six eyes, nine mouths, two ears and a horn. It is as big as a mountain and each foot covers as much ground as a thousand sheep; its task is to destroy the worst disease and pests.

The Ancient Gods

The Greek historian Herodotus commented on the ancient Persians:

The erection of statues, temples and altars is not an accepted practice among them, and anyone who does such a thing is considered a fool, because, presumably, the Persian religion is not anthropomorphic like the Greek. Zeus [i.e. God, or Ahura Mazda], in their system is the whole circle of the heavens, and they sacrifice to him from the top of mountains. They also worship the sun, moon, and earth, fire, water, and winds, which are their only original deities. . . .
Histories, I. 131, Penguin Classics, p. 68

Their altars are not to be found in temples, but high up in the mountains, and the great reliefs and inscriptions of the kings are found not in large centres of civilisation but on the rock faces of mountains.

Although the gods are often described in mythical imagery, there are remarkably few myths related about them. They may be described in anthropomorphic terms, as charioteer gods who drive forth in beautiful golden chariots pulled by immortal horses, but as soon as one looks at the anthropomorphism closely it dissolves. The great god Mithra, for example, is said to have one thousand eyes, a piece of vivid symbolism which expresses the conviction that no man can conceal his wrongdoing from the god and evade the consequences.

Many scholars believe that as Indo-European society was divided into three classes – rulers, warriors and productive workers – so too were the gods. This theory of the 'tri-partite' structure of human and divine society has been used as a key to unlock many of the problems of ancient Persian mythology – probably too many – but it is quite credible that the divine hierarchy was fashioned on the basis of the human model.

There were a great many gods in the mythology of the ancient Persians, more than can be discussed here. All we can do is to look at the main figures in Indo-Iranian and native Persian thought.

Vayu, Wind

The wind, bringer of life in the rain cloud and of death in the storm, is one of the most mysterious gods of the Indo-Iranians. In an Indian text he is said to come from the breath of the world giant out of whose body the world was made. He rides in a swift-running chariot drawn by a hundred or even a thousand horses. It is he who produces 'the ruddy lights' – the lightning – and makes the dawn appear.

In Persia he is a great yet enigmatic figure. Both the creator (Ahura Mazda) and the devil (Angra Mainyu) offer sacrifice to him. The creator

offered up a sacrifice on a golden throne under golden beams covered by a golden canopy, asking that he might smite the evil creation and that the good creation might be preserved. The prayers of the creator were granted, but the destructive desires of the devil were frustrated. Men also pray to Vayu, especially in times of peril, for he is a fearsome broad-breasted warrior. Wearing 'the raiment of warfare' and carrying a sharp spear and weapons made of gold, he pursues his enemies, to destroy the Evil Spirit and protect the good creation of Ahura Mazda.

Whereas Ahura Mazda rules above in light and Angra Mainyu below in darkness, Vayu rules in the inter-mediate space, the Void. There is a sense of the 'neutrality' of Vayu, for there is both a good and and evil Vayu. Some scholars believe that in

later thought he was divided into two figures, but in the early period there is the idea of one figure embodying the dual features of a beneficent yet sinister power, the pitiless one who is associated with death, whose paths no one can escape. If he is properly propitiated he will deliver men from all assaults, for the wind moves through both worlds, the world of the Good Spirit and the world of the Evil Spirit. He is the worker of good, the destroyer, the one who unites, the one who separates. His name is 'he that goes forwards, he that goes back-wards, he that hurls away, he that hurls down'. He is the most valiant, the strongest, the firmest and the stoutest.

Tishtrya and the Demon of Drought
Tishtrya is another figure associated with a natural phenomenon, the

rains, but there is no sense of a duality in this god's character. He is a beneficent force involved in a cosmic battle against the life-destroying demon of drought, Apaosha. Tishtrya is 'the bright and glorious star', the first star, the seed of the waters, the source of rain and fertility.

The fourth month of the year, June-July time, is dedicated to Tishtrya. In the first ten days of the month he is said to take the form of a man of fifteen – the ideal age in Persian thought. In the second ten days he takes the form of a bull and in the third ten days the form of a horse. According to the *Bundahishn* it was Tishtrya in these forms who produced the water at the beginning of creation. Each drop of rain he produced became as big as a bowl so that the earth was covered with water to the height of a man. The noxious crea-

tures were forced to go into the holes of the earth, and the wind spirit then swept the waters to the borders of the earth, thus forming the cosmic ocean.

In a hymn dedicated to Tishtrya the battle between the god and the demon of drought is retold. Tishtrya went down to the cosmic ocean in the shape of a beautiful white horse with golden ears and golden trappings. There he met the demon Apaosha in the shape of a black horse, terrifying in appearance with his black ears and tail. Hoof against hoof they fought for three days and nights, but it was Apaosha who proved the stronger, and Tishtrya 'in woe and distress' cried out to the creator, Ahura Mazda, that he was weak because men had not been offering him the proper prayers and sacrifices. The creator himself then offered a sacrifice to Tishtrya, who was infused with the strength of ten horses, ten camels, ten

bulls, ten mountains and ten rivers. Again Tishtrya and Apaosha met hoof against hoof, but this time, fortified by the power of the sacrifice, Tishtrya proved triumphant and the waters were able to flow down unrestrained to the fields and pastures. Rain clouds rising from the cosmic ocean were propelled by the wind, and the life-giving rains poured down on the seven regions of the earth.

The *Bundahishn* and the hymn to Tishtrya present Tishtrya's lifegiving act in different lights. In the *Bundahishn* Tishtrya is the primeval producer of rain, seas and lakes. In the *Yasht* the emphasis is more on Tishtrya as the continual source of water in the annual cycle of nature, the giver of offspring, the one who defeats sorcerers, the lord of all stars and the protector of the Aryan lands. The importance of the being or star who presides over the time when the rains

then can the rains give life to the world. The outcome of the cosmic battle between the forces of life and death depends on man's faithful observance of his ritual obligations.

Anahita, the Strong Undefiled Waters

It is natural that many religions should imagine the source of life and fruitfulness in female form. In Persia the goddess Ardvi Sura Anahita, the strong undefiled waters, is the source of all waters upon earth. She is the source of all fertility, purifying the seed of all males, sanctifying the womb of all females and purifying the milk in the mother's breast. From her heavenly home she is the source of the cosmic ocean. She drives a chariot pulled by four horses: wind, rain, cloud and sleet. As a source of life she is said to nurture crops and herds but also to give such material gifts as

fall can only be appreciated if one remembers the great scourge of summer heat and drought which threatens a country with vast expanses of desert.

The myth of the battle with Apaosha also tells us something of the way in which the ancient Persians viewed the ritual. They believed that the gods were strengthened and fortified by a sacrifice duly performed and offered to them. Also, by strengthening the gods the sacrifices ensured that the seasons followed their proper sequence. It is only when Tishtrya is invoked in the sacrifice that the drought is defeated; only

Above On this relief from Nimrud Dag in Commagene King Antiochus is shown shaking hands with Mithra. Whereas Herakles-Verethragna is portrayed in Greek fashion, naked, Mithra-Apollo is portrayed in typically Persian dress with cloak and leggings.

Left Detail of King Antiochus.

Opposite Detail of Mithra

horses and chariots. Because she is linked with giving life, warriors in battle pray to her for victory. She is described as strong and bright, tall and beautiful, pure and nobly born. As befits her noble birth she wears a golden crown with eight rays and a hundred stars, a golden mantle and a golden necklace around her beautiful neck.

Such vivid details suggest that from early times statues were used in her worship. Certainly they were part of her cult from the time of Artaxerxes Mnemon, for the ancient Greek historian Berossus records that the King of Kings erected statues of her in cities as far apart as Babylon, Damascus, Ecbatana, Sardis and Susa. She became a popular deity in many lands. In Armenia she was described as 'the glory and life of Armenia, the giver of life, the mother of all wisdom, the benefactress of the entire human race, the daughter of the great and mighty Aramazda (Ahura Mazda)'. (Agathangelus, quoted by Gray, *Foundations*, p. 59.)

She had many temples in Anatolia where the Roman historian Strabo says the daughters of noble families were required to practise sacred prostitution at her shrine before marriage. It is difficult to say whether or not this was practised in Persia. All the religious texts condemn prostitution in the strongest possible terms, but it has been suggested that these condemnations arose because just such a practice existed. It would be completely wrong, however, to suggest there was an orgiastic cult around the lady of the waters, for we hear of priestesses who served her taking a vow of chastity. In Persia she was, and still is, an object of deep veneration, the source of life and the object of deeply felt gratitude.

Verethraghna, Victory

Whereas Vayu and Tishtrya are associated with natural phenomena, and Anahita is thought of in personal and loving terms, Verethraghna is an abstraction, or the personification of an idea. He is the expression of the aggressive, irresistible force of victory. In the hymn dedicated to him, *Yasht 14*, Verethraghna is said to have ten incarnations or forms, each form expressing the dynamic force of the god. The first incarnation is that of a strong wind; the second is the shape of a bull with yellow ears and golden horns; the third is that of a white horse with golden trappings; the fourth that of a burden-bearing camel, sharp-toothed, stamping forward; the fifth form is that of a boar, a sharp-toothed male boar that kills at one stroke, both wrathful and strong; the sixth is that of a youth at the ideal age of fifteen; the seventh the form of a swift bird, perhaps a raven; the eighth a wild ram; the ninth that of a fighting buck, and finally, the tenth is the form of a man holding a sword with a golden blade.

The similarity between the forms of Verethraghna and Tishtrya, who both appear as man, bull and horse is obvious. How is it that in Persian thought the gods can take different forms? As we shall see in more detail later (p. 60), the Zoroastrians believe that everything in the spiritual

(*menog*) world has the faculty for possessing a material (*getig*) form. This, they believe, is how the world came to be; it was the assumption of material form by the spiritual world. But whereas terrestrial beings 'materialise under the form appropriate to their nature', heavenly or divine beings can 'materialise' under various forms – hence the three forms of Tishtrya and the ten of Verethraghna.

Unlike his Indian counterpart, Indra, or his Armenian counterpart Varhagn, the Persian Verethraghna has no myth in which he is said to defeat a monster or dragon. Instead he defeats 'the malice of men and demons' administering punishment to the untruthful and wicked. He is the strongest in strength, the most victorious in victory, the most glorious in glory. If he is offered sacrifice in the right way he gives victory in life and battle. If he is worshipped properly neither hostile armies nor plague will enter the Aryan countries. Verethraghna, then, represents an irresistible force. He is essentially a warrior god.

Two of his incarnations are particularly popular: as a great bird and as a boar. The ancient Persians viewed a raven's feathers with superstitious awe: the feathers were thought to make a man inviolable and to bring him prosperity as well as glory.

Certainly Verethraghna is said to accompany Mithra in his other form as a boar, a particularly appropriate symbol for the aggressive force of victory. In the ancient hymn to Mithra, *Yasht 10*, Verethraghna is pictured flying in front of the venerated God Mithra

in the shape of a wild, aggressive, male boar with sharp fangs and sharp tusks, a boar that kills at one blow is unapproachable, grim, speckle-faced, and strong ... has iron hind feet, iron fore-feet, iron tendons, an iron tail, and iron jaws.

On all his opponents he inflicts a gory end:

he knocks them down with a toss of his head, he cuts to pieces everything at once, mingling together on the ground the bones, the hair, the brains, and the blood of men false to the contract.
Yt. 10:70-72, AHM. pp. 107ff

It is not surprising that Verethraghna was particularly popular among soldiers, and it may have been they who carried his worship so far and wide. He lies behind the figure of Herakles at Commagene, Vahaga in Armenia, Varlagn among the Saka, Vasaga in Sogdia and Artagn in Chorasmia.

Rapithwin, Lord of the Noon-Day Heat

Rapithwin is the lord of the noon-day heat and of the summer months, the necessary beneficial contrast to Tishtrya. When the sun stood still over the world before the entry of evil it stood at the station of Rapithwin. He is, then, lord of the ideal world. In Zoroastrian belief it was at the time of day belonging to Rapithwin that Ahura Mazda performed the sacrifice which produced creation. Equally at the end of world history it will be at the time of Rapithwin – i.e., noonday – that the resurrection of the dead will be completed. Thus he is not only lord of the primeval time, but also of the renovation. He is also active year by year: each time the demon of winter invades the world Rapithwin retreats beneath the earth and keeps the subterranean waters warm so that the plants and trees do not die. His annual return to earth in spring is a foreshadowing of that final triumph of good over which he will preside. The time when evil will be ultimately defeated and God's rule on earth will be made manifest

is like the year, in which at springtime the trees have been made to blossom ... like the resurrection of the dead, new leaves are made to shoot from dry plants and trees, and springtimes are made to blossom.
Z.S. xxxiv, 0 + 27, M.B.R. p. 203

The feast of Rapithwin is part of the festival of Nauroz, the new day both of the actual year and of the future ideal time. His coming to earth is a time of joy and eschatalogical hope, a symbol of the final abiding triumph of the Good Creation.

Summary

Already we have seen something of the different characters of the ancient Persian gods. Some, such as Vayu, clearly belong to the Indo-Iranian tradition; with others, such as Rapithwin, we cannot be sure. While some, like Verethraghna, represent abstract concepts, others, such as Tishtrya, represent natural phenomena. Some, such as Anahita, are described in anthropomorphic

language; others, like Rapithwin, are not. Although there is no hint of a cosmic battle in the myth surrounding Anahita, it is very much in evidence in the myth concerning Tishtrya. There is, then, a great diversity in the concepts of the various gods.

So far little has been said of the gods of the cult. With virtually all religious traditions the ritual is the centre of the religious life, and so we turn now to the ancient Persian gods concerned with the cult.

The Gods of the Cult

Atar, Fire

To this day the fire remains the centre of certain Hindu and all Zoroastrian rites, but its origins date back to the Indo-European period. The centrality of fire is perhaps one of the best known features of Zoroastrianism. It is also one of the most misinterpreted aspects of the faith in that Zoroastrians have been labelled 'fire-worshippers' – a term they find deeply offensive. There are many layers to the traditional understanding of fire.

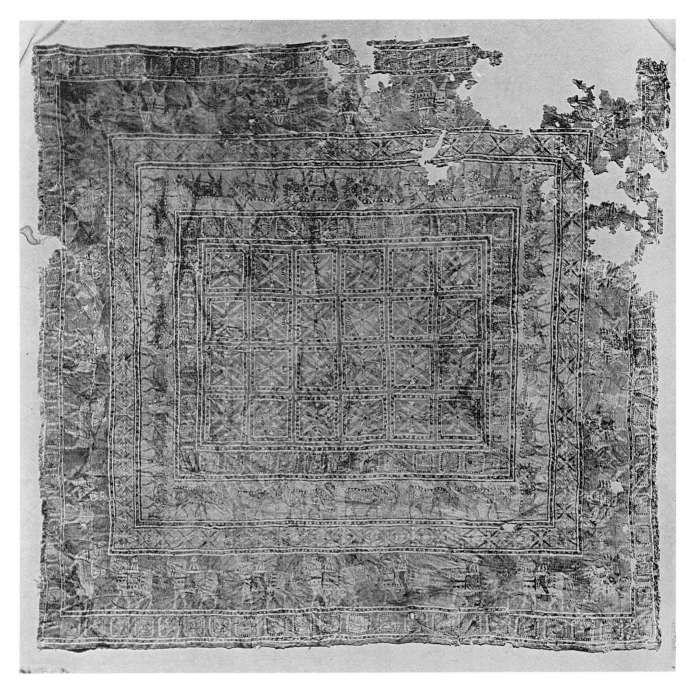

To the Indo-Iranian nomads on the Asian steppes the fire functioned not only as a source of warmth and light but also as protection against wild beasts at night. As well as being the means of cooking it was in addition part of the judicial process in that the accused was sometimes made to submit to an ordeal by fire. This took two forms, either passing between two highly banked walls of fire or having molten metal poured on the chest. In each case it was thought that God would protect the truthful and leave the wicked to their fate. All these uses of fire played a part in the development of religious imagery associated with fire. It seems that the nomads would carry fire with them in pots on their journeys rather than let it go out. These fires were used not only as hearth fires but also as ritual fires, as offerings were made to the gods on them and were seen to be carried to the skies in the flames.

In India fire is revered under the name of Agni, and is at once both earthly and divine. As sacrifices are poured on to the fire, it is thought of as a mediator between man and the gods, for it is at this point that the two worlds are brought together.

Opposite Athsho, two Kushana representations of the Persian Atar, Fire. The fire on the shoulders is probably derived from Indian imagery of Agni. On the second coin Athsho carries tongues and hammer, tools for the kindling and preservation of the fire. British Museum, London.

Above A Persian wool carpet dating from the fourth or third century B.C., the oldest knotted wool carpet known to the world. It was excavated in southern Siberia in 1949. The four-rayed star motif also appears on some Luristan bronzes. The outer borders show elks and mounted horsemen parading round the central pattern. Hermitage Museum, Leningrad.

Agni is the god who, as fire, receives the sacrifice and, as priest, offers it to the gods. The element of fire also pervades the whole universe: the sun, in highest heaven, is kindled in the storm cloud and comes down to earth as lightning where he is ever reborn by the hands of men. Agni, therefore, is described as the path to the gods, through whom the summits of heaven may be reached.

Pre-Zoroastrian Persian beliefs associated with fire provide the foundations of Zoroastrian tradition so that it is almost impossible to disentangle them in the extant texts. It seems that human imagery did not develop in Persia as it did in India, though certainly fire was thought of as the divine recipient of sacrifice and prayer. In Zoroastrianism fire is spoken of as the son of God. It is one of the seven creations, under the protection of and representing the Bounteous Immortal, Righteousness (p. 48). The ritual fire became the focal point of all Zoroastrian ceremonies (p. 124). These later Zoroastrian rites, however, reflect the ancient traditions and even use some pre-Zoroastrian hymns just as Christians use Jewish Psalms in their worship. One such prayer is the Litany to the Fire, the *Atash Nyaishe*. This is still the prayer Zoroastrians most commonly use when visiting the temple but it preserves ancient ideas of the divine recipient of prayer and sacrifice, whose blessings man seeks:

I bless the sacrifice and prayer, the good offering, and the wished-for offering, and the devotional offering (offered) unto thee, O Fire! son of Ahura Mazda.
Worthy of sacrifice art thou, worthy of prayer, Worthy of sacrifice mayest thou be, worthy of prayer, In the dwellings of men.
Happiness may there be unto that man Who verily shall sacrifice unto Thee.
Dhalla, Nyaishes, p. 155

Very few myths about Atar have come down to us, though the early Christians seem to have known of more. One myth in the ancient hymn, the *Zamyad Yasht*, tells of the struggle between Atar and the monster Azhi Dahaka (Dahak) over the Divine Glory. Azhi, three-mouthed and of evil law, the embodiment of the destructive desire, rushed to grasp the Divine Glory so that he might extinguish it. Atar also rushed to grasp and save that unattainable Glory but Azhi, charging behind, 'blasphemies outpouring', roared that if Atar seized the Glory he would rush on him and stop him from ever blazing forth on earth again. As Atar

hesitated, Azhi rushed on to seize the Glory. This time it was Atar's turn to utter threats. He warned Dahaka, 'get back you three-mouthed monster, if you seize the unattainable Glory I shall flame up your bottom and blaze through your mouth so that you will never again advance upon the Ahura created earth' (*Yt.* 19:59, based on Wolff). Terrified, Azhi in his turn drew back, and the Divine Glory remained unattainable.

What the original significance of the myth was it is hard to say, but it does show once more that the ancient Persians saw life as a battle between the forces of good and evil. Atar, naturally, fought on behalf of the good, so that in one of the Zoroastrian prayers he is called 'the bold, good warrior'. The ancient association of Fire with the natural element comes out in another late text where, as lightning, he defeats the demon who seeks to delay the rains. These myths, however, no longer play a significant part in the faith of the Zoroastrians where, as we have seen, the Fire is the symbol of Ahura Mazda and the centre of their daily devotions. The Fire, is, however, still called on as a 'warrior', for the most sacred of fires, the Bahram Fire (see p. 125) is required to do battle, not with demons of drought, but with the spiritual demons of darkness.

Haoma, Plant and God

Haoma is another Indo-Iranian figure preserved both in Zoroastrianism and, as Soma, in Hinduism. Soma is one of the main figures of Vedic ritual, where he appears as both plant and god. The juice from the pressed plant is strained through a woollen filter into vats containing milk and water. The yellow liquid is likened to the rays of the sun and the flowing liquid to the pouring rain. Soma is therefore called the Lord or King of streams and the bestower of fertility. Since the drink is thought to have medicinal power the god is said to make the blind see and the lame walk. A being of universal dominion, he gives strength to the other gods among whom he acts as priest. He is also a great fighter and the priests who drink Soma are able to slay at a glance. The plant is found on the mountains, but the celestial being, purified in heaven, stands above all the worlds.

In Persia Haoma is a plant which when pressed yielded a powerful stimulant. What that plant was in the original tradition is not known. It is described as green, with pliant shoots, fleshy and fragrant. The plant which Zoroastrians used has been identified as an ephedrin. The plant had hallucinatory properties and was thought to inspire warriors and poets. In the rituals the stems were pounded in a mortar, the juice consecrated and it was then thought to give religious insight and make the priests more open to divine promptings.

From the religious rites grew the concept of a corresponding deity: from the plant haoma grew a belief in the god Haoma. From the priestly offering of haoma developed the concept of the divine priest Haoma. As the plant had medicinal properties, so Haoma was thought to give health and strength; as haoma was thought to be the foremost of plants, so Haoma was considered provider of good harvests and sons.

The hymn to Haoma uses anthropomorphic imagery, but the invocations often blend the divinity and the herb:

Reverence to Haoma! Good is Haoma, well created is Haoma, rightly created ... healing, well formed, well working, victorious, fresh green, with pliant shoots. ... O Green One I call down your intoxication, your strength, your victory, health, healing, furtherance, increase, power for the whole body, ecstasy of all kinds. ... This first boon I ask of you, O invincible Haoma! The Paradise of the just, light, encompassing all happiness. This second boon I ask of you, O invincible Haoma! Health for this body. This third boon I ask of you. ... Long life for its vital force.
Yasna 9, 16ff, Boyce, Sources, pp. 55f

The first four men said to have pressed haoma each received the boon of a great son, Vivanghvant who had Yima, Athwya who had Thraetaona, Thrita who had Keresaspa and Pourushaspa who had Zoroaster.

In an ancient text recited during the sacrifice Haoma is besought to hurl his mace against the dragon, murderers, tyrants and harlots.

The first portion of any animal sacrifice had to be given to celestial Haoma so that as divine priest he could care for the victim's soul, and should it not be set aside the animal was thought to accuse the sacrificer at the judgment. Zoroastrians outside Iran no longer practice animal sacrifice; indeed, some would deny it was ever part of the religion, as some Christians would deny it was part of Christianity – though as Jesus and the disciples worshipped at the Jerusalem temple it obviously was. But other parts of the ancient traditions concerning Haoma have been incorporated into Zoroastrianism. One of the main temple rituals, the *yasna*, centres on the preparation of haoma. The hymns of the prophet have been described as meditations on the *yasna* (see p. 9) and it is within the prayers recited in the *yasna* that his hymns have been preserved. According to Zoroastrian belief as Haoma appeared to the prophet during the haoma ceremony, so also will Haoma be present at every offering made by the faithful. The haoma consecrated in the daily ritual is a symbol of the White Haoma which at the end of world history will make all men immortal (p. 69). It is, as it were, a foretaste of immortality. There is a direct line from ancient traditions to living Zoroastrian practice.

Summary

In Persian belief the gods are not remote beings but powers encountered directly in the ritual. The characters of Atar and Haoma also illustrate the vast difference between Eastern and Western concepts of deity. Although myths and anthropomorphic imagery are used of Atar and Haoma, they are not personalised in the way the Greeks imagined Zeus, the Jews picture Yahweh, or the Muslims describe Allah. Any similarities that occur between Persian and Christian ideas must not be allowed to cloud our vision. We are moving in a different world; Persian thought must not be viewed through Christian-coloured glasses.

Despite these remarks the heroic character of the heavenly beings does exist and is a theme which has already been noted. This is a trait which almost all ancient religions possess. In Persia there are a number of divine heroes; the stories told of them at times verge almost on the legendary rather than the mythical plane, but to omit these figures would leave a gap in our picture of ancient Persian mythology.

The Divine Heroes

Yima

Yima is another figure from Indo-Iranian belief. Although the Indian and Persian traditions agree over a number of details the general character of Yima (Yama in India) is strikingly different.

The outstanding feature of the Vedic Yama is that he was the first of the immortals to choose a mortal destiny. 'To please the gods he chose death, to please his offspring he did not choose immortality' (*RV*. 10.13.4. ZDT, p. 132). By treading the path of death he showed men the way to the path of the immortals that they might dwell with him in his abode of song. As he was the king of the dead, death became known as the path of Yama, a picture which in time came to have a rather sinister colouring, as some quite fearsome statues show.

The Persian myths, for one reason or another, have suffered in the course of transmission and it is difficult to reconstruct the total picture. Yima is most revered in Persia for his thousand-years' rule over the earth, a rule characterised by peace and plenty, where demons with all their foul works – untruth, hunger, sickness and death – held no sway. The world was so prosperous under his rule that it had to be made larger on three occasions so that at the end of his reign it was twice as large as when he began. Yima thus stands as the ideal prototype of all kings, the model for all rulers to emulate. In Persia, as in India, he appears as a king rather than as a god.

Yima is also praised for his construction of a *vara*, or cavern. Warned by the creator that three terrible winters, which will destroy all men and animals, are to befall mankind, Yima constructed a *vara* into which he took the seeds of every kind of cattle, plant and the best of men, so that the world may be repopulated after the horrors of the winter have subsided. In the later Zoroastrian texts this repopulation takes place at the end of world history. A similar myth occurs in Scandinavian belief and it may be that the two traditions have preserved, in fossilized form, myths dating back thousands of years to the time of the Indo-Europeans. Alternatively, it has been pointed out, the earliest Iranian text to include a reference to the *vara* (the *Vendidad*) was composed about the time of Christ. It may be that the Yima myth has been influenced by the Semitic tradition of the flood, one version of which is the Biblical story of Noah's ark. Perhaps the Iranians modified the myth from a story of the preservation in an ark to safety in a cavern because of Yima's long-standing associations with the underworld.

But Yima is also remembered as a sinner. Zoroaster condemned him as one who sought to please men by giving them ox flesh to eat. In other texts he is said to have been proud and to have lied by claiming divine qualities. One ancient text relates that when he began to delight in falsehood his glory flew away from him three times in the shape of a bird. The first time it was caught by Mithra, the second by Thraetaona and the third by Keresaspa. Why it left him three times we do not know, though some have suggested that it represents the three-fold structure of society over which Yima had ruled – the priests, the warriors and the artisans. The precise nature of his sin is also in doubt. It has been conjectured that a bull sacrifice, which was thought to make men immortal, was associated with Yima, thus attributing to Yima the power truly belonging to God in Zoroaster's faith, the power to make men immortal. Whether this was the

زعرغان مرآنک بدنیک سا‌ر
جوان کرد و شد مکیان و خروس
بفرمود شان تا نوار کردم
که او دامان برد ده دستگاه
جنیده به هر جای شکرکن نام
جنان بر دل هرکسی بود و داد
همه راهنگی بنوی پیشاه
برفتا هر من با فسون مست
جو دیوان بدید بند کردلو
جو طهمورث که شد زکارشان
همه بزه دیوان و افسون کران
جهان دار طهمورث به هنر بین

جوباز و جوشن بین کردن فرا
کجار خروش کنی نخم کوس
نخواند شان جز نوآرای رزم
ستایش مرا را که نبود را
نزد خبر به نیکی به هر جای کام
نماز شب و روزه آیین ستا
همه راستی خواستی پیشگاه
جو بر تیر و باز کنی بنشست
کشید ند کردن زر بازار او
براشفت و بشکست بازارشان
بزشتند جا و سپاهی کران
بیامد کمر بسته رزم کین

پیاورد و آموختن شان فرا
بیاورد یکسر بر دم کشید
جنین کفت کین پاک‌نیش کنید
مرا را یکی پاک بی‌پستور بود
همه روز پسته زخوردن دو
سرمایه بد اختر شاه ستا
جنان شاه پالو دکشتار بد
زمان تا زمان رفیش بر ساتی
شه نزد انجمن دیو بسیار مر
بزخها ندار بپشتش میان
ومنده پیسه دیوشان پیش رو

جهانی از و مانده اندر شکفت
نهفته همه سودمندی بدید
جهان آفرین را ستایش کنید
که رایش زکرد ار بدبود
به پشن جهان ارباب ی پی
دربسته بدجان بن بدخواه را
کتابیه از وفسه ایزدی
همی کرد بینش بر تاخستی
کپر دخته مانده از و پنج
کردن بر آورد کرز کرآن
همه با سمان برکشید ند غو

A seventeenth-century illustration from the *Shah-name* depicting Yima (Jamshid) on his throne ruling over a world of peace and plenty. Metropolitan Museum of Art, New York. Gift of Alexander Smith Cochran, 1913.

ancient belief we cannot really say; the later texts simply describe him as telling lies and claiming divine powers. Whatever his sin, with his glory gone Yima was left trembling in sorrow before his enemies.

The end of Yima in the Persian tradition is also something of a mystery. One old hymn says that he was cut in two by his brother, Spityura, but in later tradition it is the evil Dahak, pictured not as a mythical being but as a wicked human tyrant (Zahhak), who kills Yima and takes over his earthly realm.

Despite his sin Yima is still thought to be a figure worthy of veneration. Persepolis, the site of the great Achaemenid palace, is popularly called the throne of Jamshid (the later form of Yima's name). Yima is also credited with instituting the great annual Persian festival, *Nauroz*, an occasion for merriment and present-giving.

Hoshang and Takhmoruw

In ancient Persia there seems to have been more than one tradition about the first king, for, as well as Yima, there are two other figures called the first kings, Hoshang and Takhmoruw. The texts as we have them fit these two 'first kings' into their scheme of myth and history simply by making them into successive primeval legendary rulers, although they were once more than this.

Hoshang was ruler of the seven regions in ancient times. He ruled over men and demons; before him all sorcerers and demons fled down to darkness. Mazana was thought to be Mazanderan, whose southern boundary is marked by Mount Demavend. It is the home of many demons and sorcerers, two-thirds of whom were slain by the valiant Hoshang. His reign saw the establishment of law on earth, and from him and

his wife rose the race of the Iranians.

Takhmoruw, like Hoshang and all goodly men, defeated the demons. He attacked idolatry, wizards and witches, and propagated the true reverence for the creator. In his fight against evil he is said to have transferred the Evil Spirit into the shape of a horse and ridden him round the earth for thirty years.

Thrita, Thraetaona, Faridun

Religious traditions the world over preserve stories of battles between godly heroes and monsters. In ancient India the most famous of these is Indra, who destroyed Vritra the demon of drought with his mace, the thunderbolt, thus liberating the waters which give life to men. Another such hero is Trita, who is described in remarkably similar terms. Trita with his thunderbolt slew the three-headed, six-eyed serpent

Vrisvarupa. On another occasion Trita slew a demon in the shape of a boar with his mace. Trita roars with the storm and when he blows on them the flames of Agni rise up. But unlike Indra Trita is also remembered as a great preparer and drinker of the sacred soma.

In Persia the work of this god appears under two names, Thrita the healer and preparer of haoma, and Thraetaona (Faridun in the later texts), the one who slays the monster. Thrita was the third man who prepared haoma for the corporeal world. He prayed to the creator for a medicine that would withstand the pain, disease, rottenness, infection and death that the evil spirit was working among men by his witchcraft. In answer to Thrita's prayer the creator brought down the myriads of healing plants that grow round the Gaokerena tree in the cosmic ocean. Thrita is therefore remembered as the one who drove away sickness, fever and death from men.

Thraetaona is similarly invoked against the itch, fevers and incontinency, for all these are the work of the three-headed, three-jawed, six-eyed mighty dragon, Dahak, the lie demon whom the Evil Spirit created to slay righteousness and the settlements of men. Thraetaona is invoked against the work of Dahak for he is thought to have defeated the dragon in battle, a battle which took place in the *Varena*, or the heavens. Thraetaona clubbed the evil Dahak about the head, neck and heart but could not slay him. At last he took a sword and stabbed the monster whereupon a multitude of horrible creatures crept from his loathsome body. In fear of the world being filled with such vile creatures as snakes, toads, scorpions,

the fallen hero. Because he was triumphant over the violence of Dahak he is invoked by the faithful to repel all those who are violent.

Keresaspa

Keresaspa, the youthful hero who wore sidelocks and carried a club is another great dragon-slaying hero of ancient Persia. Like Faridun he is not recognised as a god, and so a Zoroastrian cannot pray to him, but only offer a sacrifice with a special intention for him. There were many myths, or perhaps we should call them legends, about this great adventurer, but they only exist now in fragmentary form. He is said to have defeated the 'golden-heeled' monster, Gandarewa, who rushed with open jaws to devour, whose head rose to the sun and who would devour twelve men at once. The battle with this awesome monster is said to have lasted for nine days and nights in the cosmic ocean.

Many are the monsters, highwaymen and murderers who have fallen to Keresaspa. One example is the giant bird Kamak who hovered over the earth, and whose wingspread was so great that the rain could not fall. On one occasion Keresaspa was involved in a hair-raising escapade with

> . . . the horned dragon who, horse-devourer, men-devourer, yellow and poisonous, had yellow poison mounting on him to the height of a spear.
> On the back of this dragon Keresaspa the hero happened to stew his meat in a kettle at lunch time. The monster began to be hot and perspire; he darted forth with a jolt spilling the boiling water: heroic Keresaspa fled in terror.
> Ys. 9:11, Gershevitch, IL. p. 63

It was because of his courage that Keresaspa was able to catch the glory as it fled from Yima.

At the end of the world Keresaspa will once again save men from a monster, for Dahaka will break free from his prison in the mountain. With demonic fury he will attack creation, perpetrating horrific sins and devouring one-third of the men and animals. The creator will resurrect the brave Keresaspa, who will smite the monster with his famous club and kill him, so saving mankind.

Although Keresaspa is respected for his bravery, and though he may be invoked to repel the violence of robbers, he forever remains something of a doubtful character in the Zoroastrian tradition. He was a brave, but 'devil-may-care' hero, who lacked respect for the fire, the traditional centre of the religious life, and had little concern for the religion. When at death he prayed to enter heaven, although he recounted his deeds the creator rejected him. It was only after many pleas from the weeping Keresaspa, the weeping angels, Zoroaster and the animal world that he was finally admitted.

The stories surrounding Keresaspa are good examples of the narrow line which can divide myth from legend. Although they now exist in legendary rather than mythical form, the association of Keresaspa with the end of the world may suggest that these stories once had a greater religious significance than they have now. As with many figures from the ancient lore of different nations he is remembered for his bravery, not for his misdeeds.

Summary of the Ancient Mythology

Although the ancient 'pagan' Persian belief has been preserved only in the Zoroastrian and Indian traditions, not in its own right, we can still reconstruct a great deal of the earliest Persian mythology. The ancient picture of the universe was of a flat, peaceful earth, where originally there was no evil of any kind. This state of tranquillity was shattered by the intrusion of evil which afflicted terrestrial as well as cosmic life.

As one might expect from an ancient nomadic people, the myths of the Indo-Iranians often centred on battles seen in and reflected by nature. The drought and the rains, the thunderstorm and the heat of the sun, all reflected cosmic encounters to the ancient Persians. Yet this ancient mythology cannot be described simply as a form of nature worship:

lizards, tortoises and frogs, Thraetaona refrained from cutting the monster to pieces. Instead he bound and imprisoned him in Mount Demavend, an action that mankind will one day rue, as we shall see.

His victory over Dahak gave Thraetaona the rank of the most victorious of men, apart, of course, from Zoroaster. It is because of his victorious character that Thraetaona was able to seize the glory of Yima as it fled

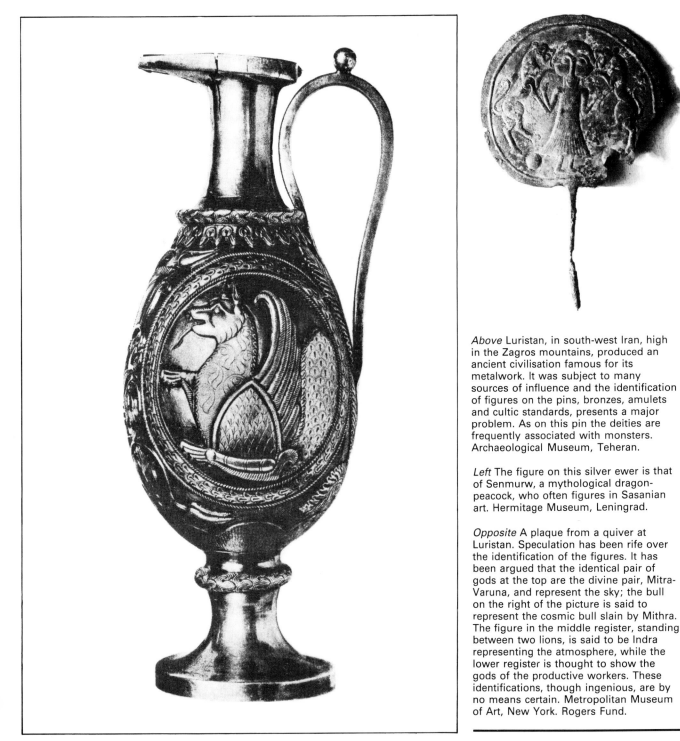

Above Luristan, in south-west Iran, high in the Zagros mountains, produced an ancient civilisation famous for its metalwork. It was subject to many sources of influence and the identification of figures on the pins, bronzes, amulets and cultic standards, presents a major problem. As on this pin the deities are frequently associated with monsters. Archaeological Museum, Teheran.

Left The figure on this silver ewer is that of Senmurw, a mythological dragon-peacock, who often figures in Sasanian art. Hermitage Museum, Leningrad.

Opposite A plaque from a quiver at Luristan. Speculation has been rife over the identification of the figures. It has been argued that the identical pair of gods at the top are the divine pair, Mitra-Varuna, and represent the sky; the bull on the right of the picture is said to represent the cosmic bull slain by Mithra. The figure in the middle register, standing between two lions, is said to be Indra representing the atmosphere, while the lower register is thought to show the gods of the productive workers. These identifications, though ingenious, are by no means certain. Metropolitan Museum of Art, New York. Rogers Fund.

some of the gods represent completely abstract ideas, such as victory, and while some gods are described in human terms, others are not.

To the ancient Persian the divine was not a distant reality far removed from human experience but a factor of everyday life. Religion was something celebrated on mountains and not in confined temples. The gods pervaded the universe; thus Atar, the son of God, is present in the heavens,

in the atmosphere and in the humble household fire. Man's daily and ritual life involves direct and immediate contact with the divine beings. The rituals were made up not only of hymns sung to distant beings – the sky, sun and stars – but also of hymns chanted to forces present in the fire and the haoma – hymns to Fire and Haoma.

Ancient Persian mythology was concerned not only with cosmic

battles, abstract concepts and ritual figures, but also with fabulous heroes, the model of kingship, the brave hero, the original medicine man. All these views of man, society, the world and the divine are expressed in ancient myths preserved by the Zoroastrians and in some cases by the Hindus. That we are able to reconstruct the beliefs of thousands of years ago is due to the intensely conservative nature of the two religious traditions.

Zoroastrian Mythology

Conflict between Gods and Demons

Dualism, the belief that there are two fundamentally opposed forces at work in the universe, is a characteristically Zoroastrian doctrine. The ancient Aryans believed in the two opposing forces of Truth or Order (Asha) and the Lie or Disorder, an idea that was taken up and developed in Zoroastrianism where the faithful are called the followers of Truth, *ashavans*, and the wicked the followers of the lie, *drugvans*.

In his hymns Zoroaster appears to assume that his hearers would be acquainted with a myth in which this dualism is cast into the form of two opposing spirits, for he says:

Then shall I speak of the two primal Spirits of existence, of whom the Very Holy thus spoke to the Evil One: 'Neither our thoughts nor teachings nor wills, neither our choices nor words nor acts, not our inner selves nor our souls agree'.
Ys. 45:2, Boyce, Sources, p. 36

This idea of the opposition of two forces was so developed in later Zoroastrianism that two distinct vocabularies were used. Thus when Zoroastrians refer to the forces of good they speak of the head, the hand, speaking and dying, but when they refer to a member of the evil forces they speak of the skull, the claw, howling and perishing.

We have already noted that to the Zoroastrians there can be no greater sin than to associate good with evil, that is, to suggest that the good world is the creation of the Evil Spirit. The opposite applies equally forcefully: there can be no greater sin than to

The Gushnasp fire, one of the three great ritual fires of ancient Persia, burned at Takht-i Sulaiman. The site itself was considered holy at least from Achaemenid times, though it is not certain that the Gushnasp fire was located there before the Sasanian period. It was housed in magnificant buildings, honoured by royal pilgrimage and gifts, and was alongside a natural deep lake so that worship was offered before two of the divine creations, fire and water. (*See also*, pages 46–7.)

The Amesha Spentas

Scriptural (Avestan) Form	Later Form	Meaning	Creation Protected	Ritually represented by
Ahura Mazda (or Spenta Mainyu)	Ohrmazd (Spenag Menog)	Wise Lord (Holy Spirit)	Mankind	The priest
Vohu Manah	Vahman	Good Mind	Cattle	Glass of milk
Asha (Vahishta)	Ardvahisht	(Best) Righteousness, Truth	Fire	Ritual Flame
(Spenta) Armaiti	Spendarmad	(Holy) Devotion	Earth	Ground of ritual setting
Khshathra (Vairya)	Shahrevar	(Desireable) Dominion	Sky (conceived of as stone or metal)	Stone pestle and mortar
Haurvatat	Hordad	Wholeness	Water	Consecrated Water
Ameretat	Amurdad	Immortality	Plants	Haoma and other plants (e.g., flowers)

associate God with evil. Good and evil are contrary realities, as are darkness and light, or life and death. They are opposing substances, not simply different aspects of the same reality. Evil is not simply the absence of good, it is a real substance and force. Good and evil cannot co-exist; they are mutually destructive and must ultimately derive from two first causes which are themselves mutually antagonistic and irreconcilable. The opposition of good and evil, or God and the devil, to use Christian terms, is the basis of all Zoroastrian mythology, theology and philosophy. To see how this is worked out we will look first at the Zoroastrians' concept of the divine and the demonic forces and then at their myths.

The Forces of Good

Ahura Mazda, the Wise Lord

Zoroaster was convinced he had seen God in visions and spoke of him as a friend. The Lord Mazda (or Wise Lord), he declared, was the father of all, the strong and holy one who established the course of the sun and stars, who upholds the earth and the heavens, the creator of light and dark, who fashioned men and creatures in the beginning by his thought; the creator both of the corporeal life and of future rewards and punishments; the creator of sleep and activity, of dawn, noon and evening; the one possessed of knowledge and father of the immortal powers.

In the later texts, where the name appears as Ohrmazd, God is often described in naturalistic terms. He wears a star-decked robe. His fairest forms are the sun on high and the light on earth; the 'swift-horsed sun' is said to be his eye. His throne is in the highest heaven, in celestial light. There he holds court, and ministering angels carry out his commands. Although this symbolism may have been taken literally by many, this must not be supposed to be the case for all Zoroastrians. Much of the mythology has, as we shall see, an abstract character.

To a Zoroastrian Ohrmazd is above all perfect goodness – he has no association with evil. Zoroastrians condemn the Christian god as evil for he allows his creation, and even his own son, to suffer. Suffering is regarded as evil for it spoils the Good Creation; it is something that God cannot yet control, but which he will one day defeat. God is the source of all that is good: light, life, beauty, joy, health. He is the power behind every throne, the inspiration of all that is true and whose earthly symbol is the righteous man.

The Amesha Spentas, Sons and Daughters of God

Zoroaster spoke of the sons and daughters of Ahura Mazda who he had created by an act of will. These six are: Vohu Manah (Good Thought); Asha Vahishta (Best Righteousness); Spenta Armaiti (Holy Devotion); Khsathra Vairya (Desirable Dominion); Haurvatat (Wholeness) and Ameretat (Immortality). Together with Ahura Mazda they are known as the Amesha Spentas, the Bounteous Immortals, a distinct group of seven who play a central role in Zoroastrian myth and ritual. Each Amesha Spenta protects and can be represented by one of the seven creations which Zoroastrians believe together constitute the divine creation, as shown on the chart accompanying the text. In the myth the Immortals care for and protect

One of the many examples of the winged symbol shown above the king on the doorways and on the walls at Persepolis. (On its symbolism, *see* page 9.)

their creations whereas in the rituals a token of each creation is present to represent the spiritual presence of that Immortal.

The abstract nature of the Immortals is immediately evident from the translations of their names. Each represents a facet of the divine nature, or an aspect of that nature in which man can and should share. It is only the creative, holy or bounteous spirit of Ahura Mazda himself which is not shared by man. Zoroastrianism, though it holds man in high esteem, never shares the idea found in Hindu-

ism of the ultimate union of man and god. Ahura is said to receive prayer and praise through each of the Immortals, but also administers rewards and punishments through them. Each can be used to represent paradise, or the good man, or the good religion. The Amesha Spentas are, therefore, the means by which God approaches man and man approaches God. So Zoroaster declares that whoever gives heed to Ahura Mazda and obeys Him will attain Wholeness and Immortality through the deeds of the Good Mind

(Ys. 45:5). It is through the Good Mind that men follow the paths of Right, gain Wholeness and Immortality and thereby attain the Dominion. Man can thus share in the nature of God; indeed, his religious duty is to be in harmony with his creator.

There has been much scholarly debate over the origin of these 'aspects'. Some believe that the figures are based on ancient gods, but whatever their source what matters most is an appreciation of the high ideals and the profound thought that they embody. In later Zoroastrianism much more picture imagery is used in association with these figures, who have been compared with the archangels of Christianity. All seven sit on golden thrones in the House of Song, the haven to which the righteous pass at death. Each of the 'Immortals' protects a part of creation: Vohu Manah protects animals, Asha the fire, Kshathra the metals, Armaiti the earth, Ameretat the plants and Haurvatat the water. Man stands under the protection of Ahura Mazda Himself. The Immortals play such an important part in Zoroastrian belief that it is worth looking at each of them.

45

Takht-i Sulaiman. (*See* also pages 42–3.)

Vohu Manah, Good Mind

Vohu Manah, the first-born of God, sits at the right hand of Ahura Mazda and acts almost as adviser. Although he protects useful animals in the world he nevertheless deals with men as well. It was Vohu Manah who appeared visibly to Zoroaster, and it is he who keeps a daily record of men's thoughts, words and deeds. At death the righteous soul is greeted by Vohu Manah and led by him to the highest heaven. Behind this picture imagery still lies the belief in the Good Mind as the personification of God's wisdom, working in man and leading man to God, for it is through the Good Mind that the knowledge of the Good Religion is attained. The demons to whom he is opposed are Aeshma (Wrath) and Az (Wrong Mindedness), but above all, Akah Manah (Vile Thoughts or Discord).

Asha, Righteousness or Truth

Asha, the most beautiful of the Immortals, represents not only the opposite of untruth, but also the divine law and moral order in the world. The believer is called an *ashavan*, a follower of Asha. Those who do not know Asha forfeit heaven, for they are outside the whole order of God. The righteous pray that they might see this heavenly sovereign so that they might follow his path and dwell in his joyous paradise. Asha preserves order on earth for he smites disease, death, fiends, sorcerers and vile creatures – all who contravene the order of the world which God wills. Asha even preserves order in hell, by seeing that the demons do not punish the wicked more than they deserve. His chief opponent is Indra, who represents the Spirit of Apostasy, for apostasy is that which draws men away from the law and order of God.

Armaiti, Devotion

Armaiti is the daughter of Ahura Mazda and sits at his left hand. As she presides over the earth she is said to give pasture to the cattle, but her true character is displayed by her name, which means Fit-mindedness, or Devotion. She is the personification of faithful obedience, religious harmony and worship. She is said to have appeared visibly to Zoroaster, an appropriate piece of symbolism in view of the prophet's faithful obedience to his call and his deep spirit of devotion. Armaiti is distressed when robbers, evil men and disrespectful wives walk free, but she rejoices when the righteous cultivate the land and rear cattle, or when a righteous son is born. Her particular opponents are Taromaiti (Presumption) and Pairimaiti (Crooked-Mindedness).

Khshathra Vairya, the Desired Kingdom

In many ways Khshathra Vairya is the most abstract of the immortals. He is the personification of God's might, majesty, dominion and power. In the celestial world this represents the kingdom of heaven, and on earth that kingdom which establishes God's will on earth by helping the poor and weak and by overcoming all evil. Because of his protection of metals he is associated with the stream of molten metal that will test all men at the end of the world. It is said, therefore, that through him God

allots final rewards and punishments. His particular opponent is Saura, the arch-demon of Misgovernment, Anarchy and Drunkenness.

Haurvatat and Ameretat, Wholeness and Immortality

Since these two feminine beings are always mentioned together in the texts, they are dealt with together here. Haurvatat, meaning wholeness, totality or fullness (often translated as Integrity), is the personification of what salvation means to the individual. Ameretat (literally deathlessness) is the other aspect of salvation, immortality. They are associated with water and vegetation; their gifts are wealth and herds of cattle, so that they represent the ideals of vigour, the sources of life and growth. Their particular opponents are Hunger and Thirst.

The Yazatas, or Worshipful Ones

The Immortals are not the only heavenly beings in Zoroastrianism. There are also the *Yazatas*, the adorable or worshipful ones. In the heavenly council the *Yazatas* rank third in importance after Ahura Mazda and the Immortals. Although in theory they are innumerable, certain figures naturally dominate, mainly those who have a particular day of the month assigned to them in the Zoroastrian calendar. The most important of them, such as Mithra or Anahita, usually have a hymn or *Yasht* of their own. Since the main *Yazatas*, Vayu, Anahita, Haoma, Atar, Verethraghna, Rapithwin and Mithra, are dealt with elsewhere in this book there is little point in giving a complete catalogue here. One important *Yazata* who has not been discussed is Sraosha. He has such an important role in myth and ritual that he merits special attention.

Sraosha, Obedience or Discipline, is one of the most popular figures in Zoroastrianism. The god is present at every divine ceremony, for he is embodied in men's prayers and hymns, and as god conveys the prayers to heaven. He is invoked in his hymn as the 'holy ritual chief'. As the Zoroastrian ritual is a potent force which destroys evil, so Sraosha is described as a warrior in armour, the best smiter of the Lie. With his battle axe he smashes the skulls of demons and hews down Angra Mainyu, but he is opposed above all to Aeshma (Fury). 'Obedience', the embodiment of the sacred word, is the victorious force in the constant battle against the destructive forces of evil. The abstract quality of the figure is obvious, but it is not denuded of mythical imagery. Thus Sraosha protects the world at night when the demons are on the prowl. He was the first to chant the *Gathas*, to spread the sacred ritual twigs, the barsom, and to offer prayer to Ahura Mazda. His house, with its thousand pillars, is on the highest peak of Mount Haraiti. It is self-lit within, and lit by the stars without. He is drawn from there in his chariot by four beautiful white horses with swift golden feet. It is he who greets and watches over the soul at death. With Mithra and Rashnu he presides over the judgment of the soul (*see* p. 64).

The mythical imagery brings out very clearly the Zoroastrian under-

Left, top The figure on this Kushana coin has been identified by a number of scholars as Vohu Manah. Sitting on a throne and holding a sceptre and diadem, the figure is one of regal power. British Museum, London.

Left, bottom Ardoxsho, a Kushana figure who has been identified as either Ashi-Oxsho, the genius of Fate or Recompense, the daughter of Ahura Mazda and sister of Mithra, Sraosha and Rashnu; or as Ardvi Vaxsha, a local eastern Persian goddess of water and moisture, related to the great Ardvi Sura Anahita. British Museum, London.

This structure, opposite the king's tombs at Naqsh-i Rustam is popularly known as the Kabah (cube) of Zoroaster. It was built by Darius in approximately 500 B.C. as a copy of one built by Cyrus at Pasargadae (popularly known as the Zendan-i Sulaiman, 'Prison of Soloman') some thirty or forty years earlier. The two buildings evidently had the same function but we do not know what that was, and there are no really similar structures to compare them with. The 'Kabah' is a little over 46 feet (14 metres) high. It is built on a three-stepped stone plinth with three rows of blind windows giving the appearance of a three-storeyed building, but it contains only one chamber which is reached by an external staircase of thirty steps (hidden from the viewpoint of this photograph). Some scholars suggest it was a fire temple or it may have housed a fire at the time of funeral ceremonies such as are still burned today near funeral grounds. But with no windows or a vent the building does not seem designed to house a burning fire. Other scholars suggest it was used as a repository for particular royal treasures, but it seems odd that any not housed in the tomb should not be kept in the nearby palace. The third suggestion is that it is the final resting place of lesser royalty, their corpses lifted up from the earth. That may be the best explanation, but it, also, remains unproven.

standing of the ritual, the stress on obedience to the divine word, obedience as the embodiment of the divine word, ritual and obedience as forces which preserve the soul and ultimately determine its fate. Obedience is not thought of as a passive quality in Zoroastrianism but rather as an active force, victorious in the fight with evil.

This is very much the picture of 'obedience' which appears in the *Gathas*. Zoroaster offers his life to God and to truth, together with his good thoughts, words and deeds, obedience and power. Similarly, obedience apportions the rewards at the end. At the outcome, at the attaining of the straight paths to Ahura Mazda, it is 'obedience' that is supreme.

On the whole the *Yazatas* tend to be either the guardian spirits of the sun, moon, stars, etc., or the personifications of such abstract ideas as blessing, truth or peace. It would be wrong, at least in the case of modern Zoroastrianism, to regard the religion as polytheistic and the *Yazatas* as gods of a pantheon like the figures of ancient Greek mythology. Zoroastrians believe that Ohrmazd is too great, too exalted for men to trouble him with their small petitions, penances or offerings. Instead they choose their own personal protector whom they approach. This does not mean that they do not revere or praise the love, power and sovereignty of Ahura Mazda, any more than a Roman Catholic loses sight of the love of God in seeking the aid and comfort of a saint. The Parsis, therefore, justifiably claim that the true parallel to the *Yazatas* are not the gods of 'pagan' pantheons, but the saints or angels of Christianity.

These then are the beings of the heavenly world in Zoroastrian belief. In short, Zoroastrians believe in one ultimate God or power, Ahura Mazda, who is absolute goodness, wisdom and knowledge, whose being man can share by partaking of the different aspects of his character, by following the path of Good Mind and Truth. His will is administered in detail by a number of 'ministering angels' who themselves are objects of love and devotion for the faithful, although none can ever replace the Wise Lord.

Opposed to the heavenly court is the world of the Evil Spirit, and it is to this that we now turn.

The Forces of Evil

Although the Persian texts leave the reader in no doubt about the horrible and vile nature of the demonic world, it is rarely described in such clear terms as the heavenly world. The arch-demons are not fitted into such a neat system as the archangels are and we are only able to reconstruct the pattern of their hierarchy because they are paired off with the heavenly beings at the end of the world. This lack of system may not be unintentional, since one of the chief characteristics of evil is its disorder and disunity.

Angra Mainyu

Angra Mainyu, or Ahriman as his name appears in the Middle Persian dialect, is the leader of the demonic hordes. Although his name does not occur as a personal name in the *Gathas*, the compound does appear and the idea of the Destructive Spirit is much in evidence. The Evil Spirit is said to have created 'non-life' (that is, a form of existence diametrically opposed to all that is good in 'real' life) and 'the Worst Existence'. Appropriately for a religion which has always taught appreciation of the good things of life, the destiny for the wicked is spoken of as 'a place of bad food'! It is 'the House of the Lie'. The forces of evil are said by Zoroaster to be the powers of Fury, Arrogance and Bad Purpose. They destroy the World of Truth, harm cattle and defraud man of the good life, and of Immortality. As Zoroaster's account of the forces of good blends myth and abstractions, so it can be seen he does also with his account of evil – so that, for example, it becomes appropriate to use capital letters for Fury and Bad Purpose as these represent both human failings and cosmic forces.

Once again, for the mythological details one has to turn to the later texts for the mythological descriptions. He is the demon of demons, and dwells in an abyss of endless darkness in the north, the traditional home of the demons. Ignorance, harmfulness and disorder are the characteristics of Ahriman. He can change his outward form and appear as a lizard, a snake or a youth. His aim is always to destroy the creation of Ohrmazd, and to this end he follows behind the creator's work, seeking to spoil it. As Ohrmazd creates life, Ahriman creates death; for health he produces disease, for beauty, ugliness. All man's ills are due entirely to Ahriman. The birth of Zoroaster was a great blow to the Evil Spirit, who tried to seduce the prophet into evil, without success. At the end of the world, despite all his efforts, it is he who will be defeated and his miscreation annihilated. It is interesting that the later texts state that the Evil Spirit has no material form. The idea appears to be that as the material world is the creation of God it must necessarily be good. Since good and evil cannot co-exist it follows that the Evil Spirit can have no material form; he can only reside like a parasite in the bodies of men and animals, and this cannot be said to be a true material existence (*see* p. 56 on evil in animal form).

Aeshma, Fury

Aeshma is the demon of wrath, fury and outrage, the personification of brutality, constantly seeking to stir up strife and war. When he fails to produce evil for the Good Creation, then he turns his attention to the Evil Creation and stirs up strife in the camp of the demons. In his assaults on men he is particularly aided by the tongues of the wicked, for they stir up anger and wrath. He accompanies those influenced by intoxicants and has as his offspring the demons of 'dishevelled hair'. His disruptive work in the world is held in check by Sraosha, the incarnation of religious obedience and devotion, the force which will ultimately rid the world of wrath.

The figure on this pin from Luristan has been identified as Sraosha, the god of obedience. The cocks' heads on the pin do suggest the association of Sraosha with the bird, but the identification of this, and many other Luristan bronzes, is rather speculative. Musées Royaux d'Art et d'Histoire, Brussels.

Mount Demavend, the mythological prison in which the demon Azhi Dahaka is bound until the end of history. It is easy to see how myths developed around this noble and mysterious mountain, which towers up to 18,000 feet (5486 metres) above sea level.

Azhi Dahaka

The term *Druj*, Lie or Deceit, is often used as a designation for Angra Mainyu or for a particular fiend, or again for a class of demons the most notorious of whom is Azhi Dahaka, a figure we have met before (p. 39). Dahaka, with his three heads, six eyes and three jaws, is painted in clearer and more mythological colours than most of the demons. His body is full of lizards, scorpions and other vile creatures so that if he were cut open the whole world would be filled with such creatures. On one occasion he offered in sacrifice to Anahita a hundred horses, a thousand oxen and ten thousand lambs, praying that he might be allowed to depopulate the earth – his constant desire. On another occasion he approached Vayu with sacrifice from his accursed palace with its golden beams, throne and canopy, but his destructive desires were scorned by both of the heavenly beings.

Filled with the urge to destroy, this offspring of the Evil Spirit sought to extinguish the sacred flame, but was foiled by the hero Yima. He had his revenge, for he not only stole the daughters of the great ruler but also sawed Yima himself in two. The sweetness of his victory was short-lived, however, for the hero Thra-etaona liberated the maidens, and imprisoned Dahaka in Mount Demavend. Here he remains until the end of history when he will again attack the world, devour one third of its creatures and smite fire, water and vegetation until he is finally slain by the resurrected Keresaspa.

The Nature of Evil

These are the three demons most clearly described; of the others we know little but their names. Even from these small crumbs of evidence, however, we can obtain a fairly clear picture of the general character of evil and its manifestations. Among the demons are Jealousy, Arrogance, Lethargy, and Wrong-mindedness. One who is often mentioned is the *Druj* Nasu, the corpse demon, who is the personification of the spirit of corruption, decomposition, conta-

gion and impurity. Another force of evil is Jahi, the demonic female embodiment of debauchery. The *Yatus*, magicians or sorcerers, are further manifestations of the disruptive forces of evil.

Although Zoroastrianism generally teaches that evil does not have physical form there are two particular forms in which man does encounter evil in the material world, that is in certain animals and in pollution.

Zoroastrianism has a doctrine of animals. Ohrmazd created animals of the Good Creation in order that they might help man. Foremost among these are the dog and cattle. The dog is considered holy because it exemplifies the religious virtues of loyalty, affection and obedience. It also plays a part in funeral ceremonies (p. 128) because in ancient Indo-Iranian myth dogs were thought to guard the entrance to the underworld. The cow is thought to be holy, as in Hinduism, because of its various products: its flesh for food; its milk for drink; its carcase for clothing; its dung for fuel and its urine for purification (with its high ammonia content it is a powerful cleansing agent). Add to these features the cow's traditionally docile nature and it can be seen why the cow became the symbol for the Good Creation and why in ancient Persian tradition the cow is used as a religious symbol, just as sheep are in the Semitic religions. Similarly the image of the herdsman is frequently used, as that of shepherd is elsewhere.

Balancing this teaching on the beneficient animals of the Good Creation, with characteristic Zoroastrian logic, is a belief in animals that are considered evil creatures, known as *khrafstras*. Any animal which shows qualities of a killer or cruelty is considered a manifestation of evil. The fly is one obvious example. Because it is found around dead matter it is linked with demons of decay and corpses. Similarly snakes and scorpions, because of their deadly bites, are considered products of Ahriman, as are dangerous man-eaters such as wolves and lions. Since beauty is a creation of Ohrmazd anything considered repulsively ugly is an expression of evil, such as a toad. It is man's duty to care for creatures of the Good Creation and to kill the *khrafstras*. There is an apparent contradiction in Zoroastrian teaching on *khrafstras* – if evil cannot have a material form, how can animals be considered evil? The answer given by one Pahlavi text is that evil had produced such potent and deadly forces that if they had remained in unseen form they would have proved particularly deadly, and therefore Ohrmazd ordered it so that they took on visible and tangible form.

In most religions and cultures there is, especially at the folk level, a strong tradition associated with ideas of purity and pollution. In Zoroastrianism such practices have been integrated into the mythical teaching on good and evil. Impurity is the form in which man commonly comes into contact with evil. The beliefs and practices proceed from the conviction that death is the work of evil and where death is present so are Ahriman and his forces. Anything which leaves the body is considered dead matter – breath, spittle, urine, faeces, cut nails and hair, and blood. Such dead matter has to be disposed of carefully so that it does not spread the pollution of death; in particular it should not be allowed to come into contact with the living or holy objects. That is why when a Zoroastrian priest serves before the sacred fire in a temple he wears a mask over his mouth, so that his expired breath, being dead, does not pollute the fire.

In the daily life of the lay person one of the most common forms in which pollution is experienced is a woman's period of menstruation, because of the dead matter within her and the loss of blood. Many religions or cultures prescribe what a woman can and cannot do at such times. The Zoroastrian teaching is based on their idea of evil. For her to enter a temple, come into contact with a fire or priest, or even with other people, including members of her own family, would be to spread the contagious pollution associated with death and the presence of evil. There is no idea of the woman being immoral: rather she is

کوشسروت

ایربرستان

کنش

ایربدان روشن

روشن تاریک

آن آموحسن

فرارون آن

آوارون فرارون

آن کار

آن آموحسن پادرهش

آن فرارون آموحسن پادرهش

the unwilling victim of the deadly assault of the Destructive Spirit. She must, therefore, live apart in a separate room or building, keeping different clothes and utensils for use at such times. On the practical side it ensures, of course, that a woman rests at a time when she needs it, but it also imposes severe social limitations on her which Zoroastrian women over the ages have borne with fortitude as their duty in the war against evil in all its forms.

Obviously the most polluting object of all is a dead body, since that represents a particular victory for Ahriman. The purity laws associated with funerals are very strict – and they will be discussed in the chapter on myth and ritual (pp. 120–133). The point about the purity laws is that they bring the cosmic conflict between good and evil into the daily lives and the homes of the believer. It is a prime Zoroastrian duty to fight evil in all its forms, wherever its corrupting influences are found – in the demons of Wrath and Arrogance, in evil creatures, in death and dirt, in the decay of rust or rotting matter.

The total character of evil, then, is negative: its aims are to destroy, corrupt and deface. Its greatest work is to bring suffering and death, the corruption and apparent destruction of God's chief creation, man. All that is horrible in man and the world, both physical and moral evil, is the work of Ahriman. The Zoroastrians do not have the theological problem of evil in the world which most monotheistic religions have to struggle with, namely: why does God allow suffering? The Zoroastrian answer is, he does not. Evil is a fact which God cannot at present control, but one day he will be victorious. History is the scene of the battle between the two forces. Let us now turn to the understanding of that history in the myths of creation, the death of the individual and the end of the world.

The Myth of Creation

Ohrmazd, dwelling on high in endless light, has no direct contact with the evil Ahriman in his deepest darkness, for between the two lies the void. The power of each, then, is limited by the other and both are spatially limited by the void. Ohrmazd is eternal, but Ahriman will one day be destroyed.

At first the two existed without coming into conflict. Although Ohrmazd in his omniscience knew of the Evil Spirit, Ahriman, ever ignorant and stupid, was not aware of the Wise Lord's existence. As soon as he saw Ohrmazd and the light, his destructive nature prompted him to attack and to destroy. Ohrmazd offered him peace if he would only praise the Good Creation. But Ahriman, judging others by himself, believed that an offer of peace could only be made from a position of weakness, so he rejected the offer and sought to destroy that which he saw. Ohrmazd knew that if the battle were to last for ever Ahriman could, indeed, keep his threat, and suggested a fixed period for the battle. Ahriman, being slow-witted, agreed and thereby ensured his ultimate downfall. The point behind this idea seems to be that if evil is allowed to operate quietly, steadily and unobtrusively it can disrupt and destroy, but once it is drawn out into the open, engaged in battle and shown for what it is, it cannot succeed.

According to the orthodox tradi-

Above A sacred bull (*varasya*) is kept in the grounds of certain Bombay fire temples. It must be white and without blemish. Its urine is used as a physical cleansing agent (*gomez*) and when consecrated (*nirang*) it is thought to help produce spiritual purity. Hairs from its tail are also used to make a ring 'filter' (*varas*) in which the haoma liquid is strained in the yasna. Only a priest of true ritual purity can consecrate the *varasya* or the *nirang*. Temples keeping such a bull supply the needs of those who do not.

Opposite Naqsh-i Rustam: Tomb in rocks. (*See* also pp. 14, 50–51, 101.)

Opposite A festive meal among Irani Zoroastrians. The author is heavily indebted to Professor Mary Boyce for her generous permission to use this and other original photographic material.

tion, history spans twelve thousand years. The first three thousand years is the period of the original creation; the second three thousand pass according to the will of Ohrmazd; the third three thousand is to be a period of the mixing of the wills of good and evil; and in the fourth period the Evil Spirit will be defeated. In the major Zoroastrian heresy, Zurvanism, the twelve thousand years are divided very differently, the first nine thousand years being the period of the rule of evil and the final three thousand the time of the defeat of evil. It may be that this second form was the older tradition.

After fixing the period for battle Ohrmazd recited the sacred prayer of Zoroastrianism, the *Ahuna Var*. On hearing this kernel of the Good Religion the Evil Spirit realised his inability to defeat the forces of good and fell back into hell where he lay unconscious for three thousand years.

Knowing that Ahriman would never change his destructive character, Ohrmazd began to create. Out of his very essence of light he produced the spiritual, or *menog*, form of the creatures. First he created the 'Immortals', then the Yazatas, and finally he began the creation of the universe: first the sky, then water, earth, the tree, the animal and, last of all, man. All these creations are completely independent of Ahriman. They are not reliant on him at all for their happiness, for Ohrmazd, unlike Ahriman, does not contemplate anything which he cannot achieve. The creatures belong entirely to God. Ohrmazd is both mother and father to creation: as mother he conceives the spiritual world and, it is said, as father he gives birth to it in material form. Ahriman in his turn creates, or rather miscreates, his own offspring from his evil nature, giving rise to all that is vile – wolves, frogs, whirlwinds, sandstorms, leprosy and so on.

The Zoroastrian creation myth is based on the ancient concept of the universe, but now it is Ohrmazd who creates the sky, which functions not only as a shell enclosing the world but also as a prison in which Ahriman is ensnared. When first produced the material creation was in an ideal state: the tree was without bark and thorn, the ox was white and shining like the moon and the archetypal man, Gayomart, was shining like the sun.

This ideal state was shattered by the onslaught of Ahriman on the world. After he had fallen unconscious into hell the demons tried to arouse him with promises of how they would assault creation and inflict on it anguish and unhappiness, but all to no avail. Then came the wicked Jahi, the personification of all female impurity. She promised to afflict the holy man and the ox with so much suffering that life would not seem worth living. She also announced her intention of attacking the water, earth, tree and fire, in fact the whole creation. Thus revived, the Evil Spirit in gratitude granted her wish that men should desire her. Then, with all the demons, Ahriman rose to attack the world. He broke through the sky which was as afraid of him 'as a sheep of a wolf'. Passing through the waters he entered the middle of the earth and assaulted the material creation. The earth became so dark that at noon it seemed like a dark night. Horrible creatures were released over the face of the earth and their pollution spread so thickly that not even as much as the point of a needle was free from their contamination. The tree was poisoned and died. Turning to the ox and Gayomart, Ahriman afflicted them with 'Greed, Needfulness, Disease, Hunger, Illness, Vice and Lethargy'. Before the Evil Spirit came to the ox Ohrmazd gave her cannabis to ease her discomfort in the throes of death, but at last her milk dried up and she died. Man, the chief ally of God and the arch-opponent of evil, was then set upon by the might of a thousand 'death-producing' demons, but even they could not kill him until his appointed time was come, for man's rule had been fixed for a period of thirty years. Everything was being destroyed, smoke and darkness were mingled with the fire, and the whole creation was disfigured. For ninety days the spiritual beings contested

with the demons in the material world. Every archangel had an opposing arch-demon, every good thing was attacked by its counterpart: Falsehood against Truth, the Spell of Sorcery against the Holy Word, Excess and Deficiency against Temperance, Idleness against Diligence, Darkness against Light, Unforgiveness against Mercy. Throughout the whole material existence and the firmament, everything was attacked and finally even man was killed.

The assault of Ahriman now seemed to be completely successful and the Good Creation to be totally ruined or destroyed. Disorderly motion, the production of evil, appeared to have won a victory over order and peace; and the work of the Wise Lord was an apparent failure.

Yet despite all appearances this was not the end of Good, for troubles were just beginning for Evil. Ahriman, after his apparent victory, sought to return to his natural home of darkness, but found his way blocked by both the Spirit of the Sky, clad in armour like a warrior, and the *fravashis* of men. The *fravashis* are a famed group in Persian mythology.

As the whole of the material creation has a spiritual origin, man has a heavenly self, his *fravashi*. Whatever evil man may do on earth his genuine heavenly self is unaffected, and it is only the earthly man, not the *fravashi*, which will suffer for his sins in hell (although one text does state that even the *fravashis* can go to hell). The host of just *fravashis* elected of their own free will to assist Ohrmazd in his battle and stood arrayed as 'valiant cavaliers with spears in hand', preventing Ahriman from escaping from the prison into which he had burst.

Thus imprisoned in a hostile world Ahriman discovered that life was beginning to flourish again. The rains were produced by Sirius; the waters washed the vile creatures into the holes in the ground, and the earth became productive. Nor was this all, for in Ahriman's apparent victory lay the seeds of his own defeat. As the ox died, fifty-five species of corn and twelve species of medicinal herbs grew from its limbs and its seed passed to the moon where it was purified, giving rise to the different species of animals. So, too, man as he

died passed seed into the earth. Thus from his body, made of metal, the earth received the different kinds of metal, and from his sperm grew the first human couple, Mashye and Mashyane.

Just as the sky, the waters (Sirius), the ox and man waged battle with the Destructive Spirit so, too, did the plants, the earth, the fire and other components of creation. Life was triumphant. Death, the work of the Evil Spirit, stood defeated, for out of death came life, and life more abundantly. From the one ox came the animals, from man the human race.

Never from the time of creation until the rehabilitation in purity has this earth been devoid of men, nor will it ever be, and the Destructive Spirit, not being good, cannot understand this will to succeed.
D.i.D. 34:2, ZDT, p. 261

Though Ahriman may kill individuals, mankind as a whole ever increases, not only rendering his assaults failures, but even making them work against him.

Man's First Parents

The first human couple grew from the seed of Gayomart which had passed into the earth. At first they grew together in the shape of a plant in such a manner that man and woman were indistinguishable. Together they formed the tree whose fruit was the ten races of mankind. When they finally assumed human form the Wise Lord instructed them in their responsibility:

You are the seed of man, you are the parents of the world, you have been given by me the best perfect

devotion; think good thoughts, speak good words, do good deeds, and do not worship the demons.
G.Bd. 14:11, BTA, p. 129

But evil lurked at hand to seduce them away from their true path. Ahriman attacked their thoughts and they uttered the first falsehood – they declared the Evil Spirit to be the creator. Attributing the origin of the world to evil was thus man's first sin; for the Zoroastrian it is the gravest sin.

From this moment on the first couple began to wander from the life God had planned for them; their orientation in life was lost. They offered a sacrifice which was not pleasing to the gods; they began to drink milk and although they shared in work – a great Zoroastrian virtue – by digging wells, smelting iron and making wooden tools, the result was

not the peace, progress and harmony which should characterise the world, but violence and malice. The demons corrupted them spiritually by inducing them to worship them rather than God, and morally by taking away their desire for intercourse for fifty years. Already in this myth we can see some of the distinctive Zoroastrian teachings emerging – the outlook on the world, on work and now on procreation. Celibacy is no virtue in Zoroastrianism; it is, indeed, the very opposite, for it fails to increase the Good Creation of the Wise Lord, thereby neglecting a fundamental religious duty of all men and women. Even when the first couple did produce offspring they devoured them until the Wise Lord took away the sweetness of children. Then, at last, Mashye and Mashyane fulfilled their function by giving birth to the whole human race.

God and Man

The world existed for six thousand years before the assault of Ahriman. For three thousand years it existed in purely spiritual form; for another three thousand it took material form, but was still combined with the spiritual. The world was created by Ohrmazd to do battle with evil. Ahriman's attack on the world produced in it all moral and physical evil. The world, plants, animals, men, even the cosmos, shook at his attack, but try as he might Ahriman could not overcome the principle of life. As the first man died he emitted seed which gave rise to the first human couple. Although they in turn were submitted to all manner of onslaughts and temptations, mankind continued to increase.

The basic conviction is that the history of the world is the history of the conflict between good and evil. In this conflict man is essentially the helper of God. He is not created for sport as in some Hindu traditions, nor as a being to whom God can manifest his glory. God needs man as man needs God. The world in which man lives, although it is defiled by the attacks of evil, is basically good. To deny this is one of the basic Zoroastrian sins. Unlike the Hellenistic religions, the Zoroastrians did not compare matter unfavourably with spirit; they held that both should be in perfect harmony for the ideal existence, towards which history moves with the end or renovation of the world.

Myths of the End

Eschatology, the doctrine of the last things, is a central and famous element of the Zoroastrian teaching. It is thought by many that this doctrine was a source of influence for both Eastern and Western beliefs – Hinduism and Buddhism in the East and Judaism and Christianity in the West.

Within Zoroastrianism there are two parts to the doctrine of the end, the end of the individual at death and the 'end' of the world. We shall look at each in turn.

Whereas belief in a life after death became a part of Jewish theology at a relatively late date, it has been a dominant part of Persian thought from earliest times. Eternity is not just a promise of a future reward; it is in fact man's true home, for that which appears to destroy man – death – is the weapon of the Evil Spirit. Man was made for life and not for death. If death were the last word then the Evil Spirit, not God, would be the ultimate victor.

It is clear that Zoroaster believed in both the individual judgment and the resurrection of the dead at the final battle between good and evil. Once again it is the later texts, however, which supply the details.

Life after death

After death the soul hovers round the body for three nights. The first night it contemplates the words of its past life, the second the thoughts, and the third the deeds. These three nights are a time of regret for the soul, regret at the death of the body, and a time of yearning for the reunification of the body with the soul. During this time the demons lurk close at hand, ever eager to inflict suffering and punishment regardless of whether it is justified. The soul, therefore, needs the protection of the just Sraosha, protection effected by the offerings and prayers of the relatives of the deceased. The three nights are also a time of anguish and consolation – anguish at the thought of the soul's misdeeds in life, consolation at the thought of its merits.

At dawn after the third night each soul proceeds to its judgment. During the life of the individual a store of merits or faults has been laid up in

the House of Song. These are weighed in the balances before the eyes of the judges, Mithra, Sraosha and Rashnu. No favour is shown on any side, either for the rich or for the poor, for the weak or for the strong. Every man is judged entirely on his own life. If the good thoughts, words and deeds outweigh the evil, the soul passes to heaven; if the evil outweigh the good, then the soul is sent to hell; but, if the two are exactly equal the soul proceeds to an intermediate place, *Hamestagan*. The Zoroastrians cannot accept the Christian idea that the life, death and sacrifice of one can atone for the sins of the many – such an outcome of the judgment would be unbecoming to the justice of a man, much less the justice of God.

As the souls leave the place of judgment they are met by a guide. The righteous are met by a fragrant wind and a maiden more beautiful than man has ever met before. Astounded at her beauty the soul asks who she is and whence she came. She replies, 'I am the Conscience of thine own self'. She is the manifestation of the soul's own thoughts, words and deeds. The wicked soul, on the other

hand, is met by a foul stench and a naked, most loathesomely diseased old hag, the manifestation of its thoughts, words and deeds.

The soul then proceeds to the *Chinvat* bridge. This bridge has two faces which it may present: to the righteous it is broad and easy to cross, to the wicked it turns and presents a sharp edge like that of a sword, so that when the soul is half way across it falls into the abyss of hell. As the righteous soul passes over the bridge it sees the spiritual *Yazatas*, the victorious Fire dispels the darkness, and spiritually purified, the soul is conducted to heaven. The wicked soul suffers great agonies; it cries and laments like a wolf trapped in a pit, but no help is forthcoming. It is compelled against its will to cross over the bridge by its evil actions, which assume the form of a wild beast that terrifies it and makes it step forward on to the bridge. Taking three steps, the steps of evil thoughts, evil words and evil deeds, it falls headlong into hell and suffers all manner of afflictions.

One barrier which wicked and righteous alike are said to face is the river of tears made by the mourners. Excessive lamentation and weeping swell the river, making it more difficult for the soul to pass over. Zoroastrians consider excessive lamentation a sin because it injures the health of the mourner, yet it is of no help to the deceased. What is much more useful is the performance of the correct rituals, for they can be of great comfort to the soul.

The After Life

We turn now to the fate of the soul after it has crossed over or fallen from the *Chinvat* bridge. But before the Zoroastrian concepts of heaven and hell are described a word needs to be said about the general picture of the after life. When the soul passes on to the place of reward or punishment it does not enter an eternal state. The idea of eternal punishment in hell is morally repugnant to a Zoroastrian, who believes that the only purpose of any just punishment is to reform or correct. A parent who punished his or her child simply for the sake of punishment would be classed as cruel. How, then, can one attribute such an action to God? Eternal suffering in hell cannot be corrective. A good god could not, therefore, allow it. Thus the Zoroastrian hell is a temporary existence where the punishment, though very severe, is a corrective one made to fit the crime, so that when good ultimately triumphs all men will be resurrected, both from heaven and hell, and the whole creation will be united with its source, the wholly good God.

Heaven

The description of heaven is contained in the writings of the righteous Viraf, who is said to have been transported in a vision to heaven and hell so that he might tell the faithful what lay before them. Led over the *Chinvat* bridge by Sraosha and other heavenly beings, he was met on the other side by the heavenly *fravashis* who conducted him to *Hamestagen*, the abode of those whose good and evil deeds are equal. Their punishment is simply from heat and cold, no more. From there he passed to the various stations of the heavens.

First Viraf went to the star station 'where good thoughts are received with hospitality'. There the souls, whose radiance glitters like the stars, sit on thrones, splendid and full of glory. At the next station, the moon station, are those with whom 'good words find hospitality'. Although these souls may not have performed all the requirements of the Zoroastrian faith they are given their place in heaven because they have performed many good works and now 'Their brightness is like unto the brightness of the moon'. The third station is that of the sun where good rulers are rewarded for their faithful administration of their heavy task. The fourth station is that of *Garodman* where Viraf was greeted by Vohu Manah, Good Mind, and led into the presence of Ahura Mazda. There Viraf was shown the different dwellings of the righteous, those who were liberal, those who were faithful in the performance of the Zoroastrian ritual and those women who had been good and faithful wives, considering their husbands as lords. Viraf was also shown the dwelling place of the agriculturalists and artisans, of those who had carried out their work faithfully, together with the places of the shepherds, the heads of villages, teachers, enquirers (into the Good Religion) and peace-seekers. All dwell among fine carpets and cushions in great pleasure and joy.

Hell

Viraf, after returning to the bridge, was then taken to hell that he might see the lot of the wicked. In the first three nights after death they suffer as much distress as a man experiences in the whole of a hard life in the world. Led by the old hag who personifies the consciences of the wicked, Viraf passed through the places of evil thought, evil words and evil deeds into hell. There he experienced intense cold and heat, darkness so intense that it could be grasped and a stench so powerful that it could be cut with a knife. He saw the 'greedy jaws of hell, like the most frightful pit'. Everyone in hell is packed in so tight that life is intolerable, yet all believe that they are alone and time drags so slowly that after three days

Above The 'tower of silence' or *daxma* from Karachi. The photograph, *opposite*, shows the actual *daxma* with steps leading up to the door where the corpse-bearers, and they alone, carry the body. The mourners take their final leave of the body at the horizontal marble slab in the foreground where it is laid for a few moments. Traditionally *daxmas* should be on a remote and barren hill. That was not possible in Karachi though the hillside is

they believe that the nine-thousand-year period of the world has elapsed. Everywhere there are vile creatures seemingly as high as mountains, which tear and seize the souls of the wicked. The miserable wretches suffer from the extremes of driving snow and the heat of the brisk-burning fire, from foul stench, stones and ashes.

Each soul is subjected to severe, appropriate, punishment for its misdeeds.

A woman who had committed adultery was suspended by the breasts to hell; and noxious creatures seized her whole body.
AV. 24, Haug, p. 171

A man who had given false measure in trading they ever forced to measure dust and ashes, and they ever gave him to eat.
AV. 27, Haug, p. 172

A ruler who was unmerciful was held in the atmosphere, and fifty demons ever flogged before and behind, with darting serpents.
AV. 28, Haug, p. 173

A man who had ever been selfish with many riches remained stretched on a rack, and a thousand demons trampled upon him with great brutality and violence.
AV. 31, p. 174

The individual punishments are ameliorated according to the good deeds performed. Thus a man who had committed adultery was set in a boiling cauldron, but because he had killed many vile creatures with his foot this was left outside the cauldron and did not suffer like the rest of his body.

These texts are interesting not only for their general picture of heaven and hell as a place of stern but corrective punishment, but also for the details given of what a Zoroastrian considers to be a religious sin: giving false measure, unjust rule by a monarch, a woman having an abortion, homosexuality, and so on.

Both heaven and hell are here described in material terms. Heaven is above the earth and hell under the earth. The delights and torments are also described in physical terms. Yet the texts stress that the delights and sufferings far exceed anything which is experienced on earth, and in view of the stress on the *soul's* experiences it may be that this post-mortem fate was thought of as a spiritual experience, even though there was no language to express it as such. As we have seen, ancient Persian myths are often vivid expressions of abstract ideas.

left barren as far as possible from human habitation. The photograph *above* was taken from the steps of the building *opposite*, the place where the bereaved go to offer prayers as the corpse is taken into the *daxma*. This relatively modern structure, like Zoroastrian art through the ages, reproduces stylistic features from Persepolis, compare, for example, the crenellations on the main roof with those on the palace walls shown on page 96.

The Universal Judgment

As we have seen, the Zoroastrians believe that the history of the world lasts for twelve thousand years. The final period in which evil is defeated is thought to have started with the birth of Zoroaster, so that in Zoroastrian belief we are living in the final period of world history.

The final period of history is itself divided into four lesser periods, each being symbolised by a metal: gold for the period when the Good Religion was revealed to Zoroaster, silver for the period when his royal patron accepted the religion, steel for the Sasanian period and iron for this present age when the religion is declining. Although it is in this period that evil is defeated the battle is not one long success story for the forces of good, but a series of pendulum swings when first good and then evil appears to be triumphant. During this final world age of three thousand years the Zoroastrians expect three saviours to come, at one-thousand-year intervals. The first was expected a thousand years after Zoroaster. Since Zoroaster is said in some Pahlavi sources to have lived about 600 B.C. (historians prefer an earlier date) this means that the first two saviours should have made their appearance by now. How Zoroastrians overcome this problem we shall see later. They believe that the period of iron, the period of the decline of the religion before the appearance of the first saviour, still continues.

The Period of Iron

This period is marked by what the Judeo-Christian tradition calls the 'signs of the end' – manifestations of the horror and power of evil. Demons of the race of Aeshma (Fury) with their 'dishevelled hair' will attack Persia. The result will be the complete destruction of ordered life in the land. Family and social life will disintegrate, and the respect for truth, love and the Good Religion will decline. The disruption will be cosmic also: the sun and moon will not give their proper light; there will be darkness and gloom on earth, earthquakes, droughts and famine. There will be battles on earth and life appears to be so horrible that Zoroaster, to whom all this is said to be revealed in a vision, prays that he may not live at that time. This onslaught of evil is parallel to that at the beginning of world history. Then the Evil Spirit afflicted the sun, shook the earth so that mountains appeared and inflicted disorder on order. Similarly at the end, the sun's light will be affected, earthquakes will break out and family, social and religious life will be rendered chaotic.

At last a shower of stars will appear in the sky, marking the birth of a righteous prince who will overcome the evil armies and restore the Persian lands and throne of the Good Religion prior to the birth of the first saviour.

The First Saviour

The saviour, Aushedar, 'the developer of righteousness', though he is to be born of a virgin, will also be the offspring of the great prophet, Zoroaster. The myth relates that Zoroaster's seed has been preserved in a lake. At the approach of the millennium his seed will impregnate a fifteen-year-old virgin while she is bathing and the saviour will be conceived.

When he reaches the age of thirty the sun will stand still for ten days at the noon-day position, Rapithwin, where it had stood before the first attack of Ahriman. The saviour will confer with the archangels, and he will bring with him the revelation first brought by Zoroaster. Through his coming something of the paradisal state returns. For three years men will live more harmoniously and part of the evil creation, the wolf species, will disappear. Thus the coming of the first saviour gives the first foretaste of the perfection to come, the combination of primeval order with the Good Religion brought by Zoroaster. The renovation of the universe is not, however, complete. For evil will still exist and will assert itself once more.

The texts do not agree over the nature of the outbreak of evil which will occur at the end of this millennium. Some state that the enemies of Persia will return and suppress the Good Religion and the state, but this appears to be a historicising of the mythical belief contained in other texts where the outbreak of evil takes the form of a terrible winter produced through the sorcery of the demon Malkus. The snow and hail will destroy a large part of mankind. Yet before the coming of the second saviour good will again triumph for the earth will be re-peopled from the *vara* built by Yima (see p. 34). In this re-populated earth disease will no longer prove fatal and death will come about only through old age or murder. Thus Ahriman's greatest weapon, death, will begin to lose its

This stone relief showing magi in connection with animal sacrifice dates from the fifth century B.C. and comes from Dascylium, or Eregli, in Asia Minor. The various accurate details, the covering over the mouth, the priestly emblem of the barsom twigs and the setting apart of the head of the sacrificial animal, illustrate how widespread was the knowledge of Zoroastrian priestly practices. Many modern Zoroastrians, notably Parsis, vigorously deny animal sacrifice was ever part of the religion, and certainly do not practice it now. There was a logic to the practice however: since mankind eats meat, it is a religious duty to ensure that animals, man's fellow workers, die with merciful swiftness. Hence there was no public abattoire; instead a compassionate priest accepted responsibility and offered the first portion, the head, to spiritual beings.
Archaeological Museum, Istanbul.

power prior to the birth of the second saviour.

The Second Saviour
Like his predecessor, the second saviour, Aushedar-mah, will be born of a virgin who has been impregnated by the seed of Zoroaster preserved in a lake. Whereas the sun stood still for ten days at the coming of Aushedar it will now stand at the noonday position for twenty days and the creation will flourish for six instead of three years. During the millennium of Aushedar wolves had disappeared from the face of the earth and now more members of the evil creation will disappear, snakes for instance. The original paradisal state will draw yet nearer. Men will no longer need to eat meat, they will become vegetarians and drink only water.

But despite this growing power of the Good Creation and the gradual expulsion of evil, the powers of darkness are far from finished. Evil will re-assert itself in the form of Azhi Dahaka, the monster who had been imprisoned in a cave in Mount Demavend by Thraetaona (see p. 40). He will escape and rushing into the world will perpetrate sin, devouring one-third of mankind and the animal world. He will smite the sacred elements of the fire, water and vegetation. But another ancient hero, Keresaspa, will be resurrected and will rid the world of this evil being.

The millennium of each saviour thus follows a neat pattern: prior to the saviour's birth good will be in the ascendant, the miraculous appearance of the saviour will bring creation nearer to the paradisal state and the powers of evil will be reduced. Yet evil will, on each occasion, launch an assault which threatens to destroy mankind until it is overcome through the work of one of the primeval heroes.

The Third and Final Saviour
Soshyant, the final saviour, will be conceived by a virgin in the same way as his predecessors, but with his coming the complete and final triumph of good will arrive. All disease, death and persecution will be overcome, vegetation will flourish perpetually and mankind will eat only spiritual food. The world is now to be perfectly and finally renovated. The dead will be raised by Soshyant from the spot where life had departed from them. All men will then proceed to the last judgment where everyone will see his good and evil deeds. There the righteous will appear as conspicuous among the wicked as white sheep are among black. After this judgment the wicked will return to hell and the righteous to heaven for a period of three days and three nights to receive their due reward. Whereas the bridge-judgment, with its ensuing reward or punishment, was concerned with the soul, the last judgment, following the resurrection, will be concerned with the whole man, body and soul, so that finally man may praise the creator in his total being, in the perfect harmony of spirit and matter. First, however, all men will have to pass through a stream of molten metal. The stream of metal which has already levelled the earth to its primeval state of a plain will sweep over all men that they, too, may be made uniform in purity. The gift of immortality will be conferred when Soshyant, acting as priest, celebrates the final sacrifice with the last animal to die in the service of man, the ox whose role in primeval history we have already noted. From the fat of that ox and the mythical White Hom from the cosmic

ocean the elixir of immortality will be prepared.

The texts then relate the final defeat of evil, although this may not have been the chronological position the event held in Zoroastrian belief. Each of the heavenly beings will seize and destroy his demonic opponent until the only survivors, Ahriman and Az, flee back to hell. The molten metal which has levelled the earth and swept over men will flow into hell, consuming the stench and contamination which characterises that place, so that all evil will be rendered impotent if not annihilated. Unfortunately the texts are not clear on Ahriman's precise fate. The hole which the Evil Spirit had made on his entry into the world will be sealed up. With the earth levelled and man restored to his ideal unity of body and soul the whole creation will be once more the perfect combination of spirit and matter that God intended it to be.

It is wrong to call this event the end of the world, for in Zoroastrianism it is not that. The end of the world would be the victory of Ahriman. It is rather, as the Zoroastrians themselves call it, the Renovation. The world is restored to the perfect state it enjoyed before the assault of Ahriman. But it is even more than that. Matters have not simply returned to their former state, for now Ahriman is no more and Ohrmazd reigns, not only all good, all knowing, but now all powerful also.

The Continuity of Traditions

It is convenient and helpful in books like this to divide the subject matter into sections, in this case 'Ancient' Persian mythology and 'Zoroastrian' mythology. There is some truth in these divisions because religions do change with the passage of time. Change may be essential for continuity in a religion; if a religion did not adapt to new patterns of thought, to developing climates of opinion, it would no longer be meaningful to its adherents and would cease to be a living religion. Religious teachers reflect upon and interpret the received

Rustam, a legendary hero of Persian tradition, defeats the proud Turanian warrior, Puladvand. (*See also* pages 118–119.)

tradition. This is true of Zoroastrian teachers. The pattern of three saviours outlined in the last few pages is probably an example of priestly elaboration of earlier ideas. But what is striking about the mythologies of most religions, especially Zoroastrianism, is their timeless quality, and the faithfulness with which the basic themes and principles are preserved and handed on from generation to generation. It would be impossible to understand Jewish and Christian teaching without a real knowledge of Biblical mythology. Equally one cannot appreciate Zoroastrian teachings without an understanding of ancient Persian myths. The two are not different subjects; one is founded upon and continuous with the other.

It was once fashionable among scholars to emphasise the difference between what was said to be the abstract philosophical teaching of Zoroaster and the mythical beliefs of his later followers. In fact what seems to have been the case is that Zoroaster shared the same basic myths as his predecessors and followers, but in the small fragment of his teaching which has survived the emphasis is on applying the personal or moral implications of known myths to the lives of his hearers. A good example from the *Gathas* is *Yasna 30* where the prophet addresses an obviously well informed group of hearers and applies to their lives the evidently well known myth of the choice of the twin spirits (Ahura Mazda and Angra Mainyu). Like many a modern preacher Zoroaster exhorts his listeners to choose between the paths

of good and evil, to declare themselves for God before judgment day comes:

Truly for seekers I shall speak of those things to be pondered, even by one who already knows. . . . Hear with your ears the best things. Reflect with clear purpose, each man for himself, on the two choices for decision, being alert indeed to declare yourselves for Him [i.e., Ahura Mazda] before the great requital. Truly there are two primal Spirits, twins renowned to be in conflict. In thought and word, in act they are two: the better and the bad. And those who act well have chosen rightly between these two, not so the evildoers. . . . Of these two Spirits the Wicked One chose achieving the worst things. The Most Holy Spirit . . . chose right, and so do those who shall satisfy Lord Mazda
Boyce, Sources, p. 35

This text illustrates clearly both Zoroaster's acceptance of the traditional myths and the way in which religious teachers use myths in their preaching as stories full of significance and meaning for the individual's life.

Zurvanism,
A
Zoroastrian
Heresy

So far in this book attention has been focused on the orthodox teaching and mythology of Zoroastrianism. Even the ancient beliefs that have been expounded are preserved only in Zoroastrian texts and they themselves have been incorporated into the Zoroastrian system. But, as with any religion, different beliefs and mythologies grew in Zoroastrianism, the main dissident group being the Zurvanites.

Although some scholars believe Zurvanism to be a pre-Zoroastrian tradition, it is usually thought that it developed during the Achaemenid period as a result of Babylonian influence. It may have been very popular during the Parthian period when it seems to have exerted influence on a number of Western traditions, notably certain aspects of Judaism and Gnosticism. But it was during the Sasanian period that it appears to have come to the forefront of Persian religious life, lasting into Muslim times. Even during the Sasanian period, however, it probably flourished as an intellectual movement within the Zoroastrian Church, rather than as a distinct sect. Zurvanite mythology is very difficult to reconstruct as we have no purely Zurvanite text, only the accounts of outside observers and the occasional polemic of Zoroastrians. Such evidence must obviously be used with caution.

The name of the 'sect' is derived from their name for the ultimate being, Zurvan, Time. Zurvan, they believed, was the ultimate source of both good and evil, the Father of the brothers Ohrmazd and Ahriman. In Zurvanite belief the Absolute contained within his being the polarity of good and evil. The Zurvanites sought a unity behind the dualism of orthodox Zoroastrianism. The implications they drew from this belief were enormous, but before discussing these we shall set out the myth as it is preserved in the reports of foreigners, principally Eznik, an Armenian.

Before the existence of earth or heaven the great and ultimate being Zurvan existed alone. Wanting a son he offered sacrifice for a thousand years. The offering of sacrifice does not imply that he was praying to any other being, for in Persian belief the offering of sacrifice has merit or power in and of itself. After a thousand years, however, he began to doubt the fulfilment of his desire. He doubted the power of sacrifice to produce a son, Ohrmazd, who would create the heavens and the earth. At the moment of his doubt twins were conceived within himself, for Zurvan, being the undifferentiated one was androgynous. The twins were Ohrmazd, the fulfilment of his desire, and Ahriman, the personification of his doubt. Zurvan vowed that he would give the gift of kingship to whichever son emerged from the womb first. Ohrmazd, already displaying his great characteristic of omniscience, was aware of this and informed his brother, whereupon Ahriman ripped open the womb, presented himself to his father, declaring 'I am your son Ohrmazd.'

And Zurvan said: 'My son is light and fragrant, but thou art dark and stinking.' And he wept most bitterly. ZDT. p. 208

When Ohrmazd appeared Zurvan recognised him immediately as the fulfilment of his desire and offered him the symbol of priesthood, the barsom twigs. In order that he should not break his vow of the gift of kingship for the first born, he gave Ahriman the rule of the world for a period of nine thousand years. To Ohrmazd he granted rule above so that Ohrmazd created the heavens and the earth.

Ahriman, meanwhile, as in orthodox Zoroastrianism, created the demons, poverty and all that is evil and perverse. Ohrmazd represents all that is good in Zurvan, Ahriman all that is evil. Behind the manifold experiences and features of life the Zurvanites saw one ultimate source which encompassed all within the one being, the polarity of light and dark, good and evil. Evil exists in the world not as a result of error, nor ultimately as the miscreation of the Evil Spirit, but as a potentiality within the nature of the Absolute. The purpose of the battle between good and evil is to restore the unity within the Absolute which was shattered by divine doubt.

The implications drawn from this myth were mainly of a philosophical nature and because of this it has been plausibly argued that Zurvanism was mainly the religion of the intelligentsia. There appears to have been more than one form of Zurvanism, but whether these differences ever gave rise to distinct sects of Zurvanism is rather unlikely.

One of the developments of the belief in Zurvan was the idea of a materialistic evolution of the universe, a development which may have taken place under foreign influence. The idea was that the creation of the universe was not an act of God but an evolutionary development of formless primeval matter, Infinite Time and Space (Zurvan) into all that has form, the finite. The Infinite thus becomes the finite. This process can, of course, stand without belief in a creator and it seems that with this 'evolutionary' idea went a denial of heaven, hell and all future rewards or punishments. In short, this attribution of the evolution of the world from the primal Time/Space, Zurvan, was based on a thoroughly materialistic interpret-

Above The figure on this Luristan bronze has been identified as Zurvan giving birth to twins, Ohrmazd and Ahriman, surrounded by the three ages of man: youth (bottom left) maturity (left) and old age (right). The figures are said to be holding the sacred barsom twigs. This may be an anachronistic interpretation. Perhaps the myth underlying the scene developed into the Zurvanite myth.

Right This Luristan bronze is thought by some to portray Zurvan, flanked by the two spirits, Ohrmazd and Ahriman. However, it is by no means certain whether the Zurvanite myth dates back to this early period.

ation of the universe, fundamentally alien to the orthodox Zoroastrian belief in a creator, a life after death and a stress on rewards or punishments.

The evolution of the world from Time was taken by some to imply that the world was bounded and controlled by the heavenly sphere. In terms of astrological myth this meant that the fate of the individual was pre-determined by the cosmic battle between the twelve signs of the Zodiac, representing the forces of good, and the seven planets which oppress creation by ruling over its fate. This fatalism, foreign to orthodox Zoroastrianism, exerted quite a degree of influence in Persian thought. It not only entered some Zoroastrian writings, but also appears in some passages of the vast epic, the *Shah name*. The poet recounts the questioning of one Zal by the Magian hierarchy. As a test of his religious knowledge he has to interpret a set of riddles. One such is about a man who

with a great sharp scythe strides insolently towards the meadow (full of greenery and streams). Moist and dry he mows down, and if thou make supplication he will not hear thee.

The interpretation of this riddle is that the man with the scythe is Time, and we are the grass. All are treated alike by the mower; no account is taken of youth or old age, all in his path are cut down. The nature of the world is such that if it were not for death in the world there would be no birth either.

We enter in at one door and pass out of another: Time counts our every breath.
ZDT. pp. 240f

This gloomy outlook on life, the cynical attitude to birth and death are far removed from the optimistic, positive attitude of orthodox Zoroastrians.

A cynical attitude to women is thought by many to have been another feature of Zurvanism. In some reconstructions of the Zur-vanite account of evil's entry into the world the evil Jahi, the whore, first united herself with Ahriman and then seduced the righteous man, Gayomart. If this was so then the Zurvanites believed that it was woman's sexual desire which was the cause of evil in the world. According to one Zoroastrian text, the *Bunda-hishn*, Ohrmazd admits that, although women are helpful to him because they give birth to men, he would never have created women if he could have found any other vessel. But search as he did in the waters and the earth, among plants and cattle, in the mountains and valleys, he could find no alternative. This is often taken as an example of Zurvanite influence on Zoroastrianism. It may also be, of course, that there were misogynists and 'oddities' among traditional Zoroastrians and that this was not a specifically Zurvanite belief. Such phenomena exist in most religions – Christianity has never been lacking in this respect despite the importance of Mary – so the same may apply to Zoroastrianism. There is a great danger in labelling every unusual Zoroastrian belief 'Zurvanite'.

The main differences between Zurvanism and Zoroastrianism, then, are those based on the idea of the Absolute as Infinite Space/Time, the nature of Zurvan, the belief in Ohrmazd and Ahriman as twins, the idea that Ahriman ruled the world for nine thousand years, fatalism and materialism.

The Mythology of Mithraism

Mithra is an important god in the history of many different countries at many different times; his worship spread as far west as the north of England and as far east as India. First worshipped thousands of years ago, he is still venerated by Zoroastrians today.

In ancient India where his name appears as Mitra, translated as either Friendship or Contract, he was usually invoked with another god, Varuna, True Speech, in the formula Mitra-Varuna. The two are often described in human terms. Together they mount their shining chariot, which has the trappings of any earthly chariot. They dwell in a golden mansion which has a thousand pillars and a thousand doors. But despite this imagery there are no stories or myths told about them. The imagery is used simply to draw out the character of these two figures.

Mitra and Varuna are described as cosmic rulers upholding order in the world of gods and men, for Contract and True Speech are the basis of all ordered life in the cosmos, in religion and in society. Through the observance of the Contract mankind is united and falsehood overcome, and by faithful fulfilment of one's ritual duties the sun is made to shine and the rains to fall.

From Persia we have a hymn to Mithra which is usually dated about 450 B.C. in its present form, although the material it uses is much older than this. As in India Mithra has a great palace, one built by the creator in which there is

no night or darkness, no wind cold or hot, no deadly illness, no defilement produced by evil gods.
Yt. 10:49-50 AHM p. 99

Mithra rides forth in his chariot pulled by four white immortal horses shod in gold and silver. He is

the first supernatural god to approach across the Hara, in front of the immortal swift-horsed sun ... the first to seize the beautiful gold-painted mountain tops, from there the most mighty surveys the whole land inhabited by Iranians.
Yt. 10, 12-13, AHM p. 79

In Persia, as in India, the mythical imagery is used only to bring out the character of the god Contract. Mithra is the one who preserved Order or Truth. He it is who attacks and defeats the demons of the Lie; he it is who judges when the contract concerning the different periods of world history is completed. In his concern for Truth he judges the soul at death and brandishes his mace over hell three times each day so that the demons do not inflict greater punishment on sinners than they deserve. One scholar who lived among Zoroastrians for some time tells how a Parsi mother in Karachi, finding one of her grandchildren fibbing, admonished him to remember that Mithra was watching and would know the truth.

The hymn to Mithra expresses this idea of the god Contract preserving Truth and Order in the picture imagery of a 'mighty strong warrior' with a pike of silver, gold armour, an iron mace with one hundred bosses and blades, and strong shoulders smashing the heads of evil gods and men, before whom

the Fiendish Spirit ... malignant Wrath ... long-handed Procrastination ... all supernatural evil gods ... recoil in fear.
st. 97 AHM p. 121

The marble relief from the Walbrook
Mithraeum in London. Instead of the
cosmic cave which usually provides the
setting for the main bull-slaying scene,
this monument uses the circle of the
zodiac to emphasise the cosmic
dimension of Mithra's work. This is further
emphasised by the ascending (left) and
descending chariots of the sun and moon
and below the busts of two winds. An
inscription states that it was dedicated by
a veteran of Legion II Augusta. It
probably dates from the third century.
The Museum of London.

To the Persians Persia was naturally the land of the Contract and we find that before going into battle against 'anti-Mithraean countries' the soldiers prayed to Mithra 'at the manes of their horses' and a Roman historian records that before going into battle the Persian King

with his generals and staff passed around the ranks of the armed men, praying to the sun and Mithra and the sacred eternal fire.
Quintius Rufus, History of Alexander, IV, 13, 2

Mithra continues to play an important part in living Zoroastrianism. The correct term for a temple is *dar-i Mihr*, the gate or court of Mithra. When a priest is initiated he is invested with a *gurz*, the mace of Mithra as a symbol of his priestly duty to make war on evil. All the most sacred rituals are offered under Mithra's protection and one of the great Zoroastrian festivals, still celebrated in modern Persia, is the *Mihragan*, a festival in honour of Mithra, Judge of Iran, for a period of five days with great rejoicing and in a spirit of deep devotion.

Mithra (now with an 's' — 'Mithras') was also an important Roman god. Just how this came about is not really known — but it is one of the great ironies of history that Romans worshipped the god of their chief political enemy, Persia. Scholars presume that Persians living in the satellite countries of Pontus, Cappadocia and Commagene — where pockets of Persian traditions were retained from the times of conquest by the Kings of Kings — were recruited into the Roman legions and then transferred across the empire carrying the worship of the Persian god with them. In Hellenistic and Roman times the Western image of Persia was of a land of mystery, wisdom and learning so that its religious teachings appealed to those who found the

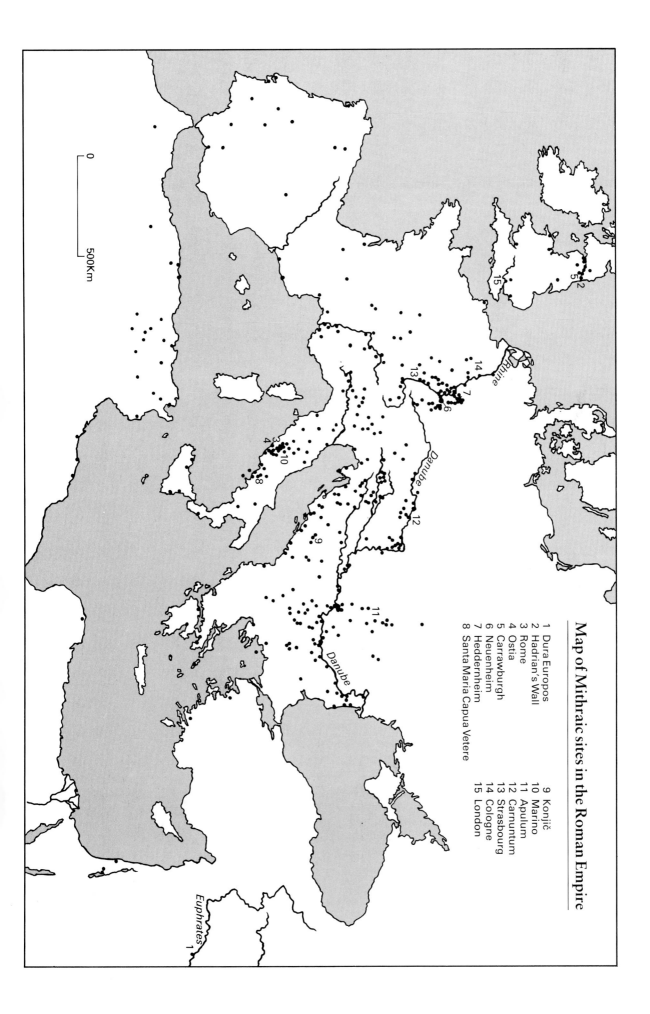

Map of Mithraic sites in the Roman Empire

1 Dura Europos
2 Hadrian's Wall
3 Rome
4 Ostia
5 Carrawburgh
6 Neuenheim
7 Heddernheim
8 Santa Maria Capua Vetere

9   Konjič
10 Marino
11 Apulum
12 Carnuntum
13 Strasbourg
14 Cologne
15 London

established state religion uninspiring – much as in the 1960s and 1970s many western university students turned to Indian religions as an oriental source of spirituality.

The Roman cult of Mithras flourished for approximately three hundred years from about A.D 100 to 400 (precise dates are impossible). It has been said that Mithraism was so strong that if the Roman Empire, and after it the Western world, had not become Christian it would have become Mithraic. This is a gross exaggeration, but undoubtedly it was a powerful cult, popular particularly among the soldiers and so found in frontier regions such as the Danube and Rhine valleys, but also along Hadrian's Wall in the north of England. But it was also found among the civilian population, notably in Italy, especially Rome and her port of Ostia, and in eastern Europe in the countries now known as Rumania, Hungary and Bulgaria. Mithraic sites have been found as far east as Israel and Syria and in north Africa. The evidence from inscriptions in temples

and on altars is that it was a socially respectable movement with high military officers, even Emperors, dedicating buildings and objects to Mithras.

Mithraism was known to its contemporaries as 'the Persian Mysteries', and Mithras himself was referred to as 'the Persian god'. Some explicitly attributed Mithraic teachings to Zoroaster. The Persian origins appear to be confirmed by some of the details in the Mysteries; there are, for example, recognisably Persian words used and one of the seven grades of initiation is that of the Persian. Scholars have, therefore, often conflated the evidence of Persian texts with that of Roman archaeological finds – because there are practically no written sources from within the cult in the Roman empire.

The usual interpretation of Mithraic art is to see it depicting the life of the god. He is shown being born as a young man (never as a baby), emerging either from a rock or the zodiac, holding a torch

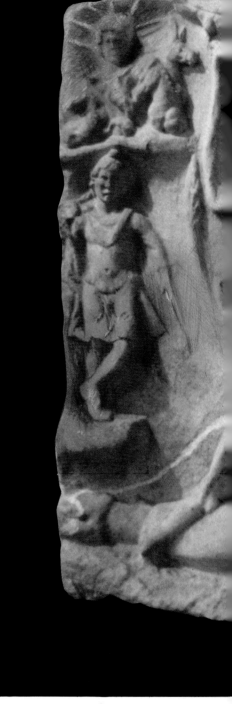

Above left The finds from the first Mithraeum at Heddernheim, as displayed in the Städtisches Museum, Wiesbaden. The reliefs of the torchbearers and the statues of the lions were placed to the sides of a central aisle, but their precise function is not known. The central panel of the relief swivels; on the reverse is a scene of Mithras and Sol sharing a meal over the body of the bull. It is presumed that the relief was swung round at a set

point in the ritual. This is one of the most famous, and detailed, of all the cult reliefs. Its composition, with regular panels at each side and along the top, is characteristic of a number of reliefs from the Rhine region, a pattern reproduced in some painted Italian Mithraea. (*See* for example, pages 82 and 87). It used to be thought these panels could be read rather like a comic strip, following a story line. Recent research has shown this not to be the case; rather scenes were intended to balance each other on opposite sides of the relief.

Above A Mithraic relief found in the 1970s near Dunaujváros in Hungary. Recent studies have tended to emphasise the importance of the finds in central and eastern Europe, and it is likely that further research in that area will advance the subject considerably.

representing the sun or the knife with which he will later slay the bull. In the panel scenes to the side of some carved reliefs Mithras is shown shooting an arrow into a rock (or cloud) to release the waters for his followers. On others he is shown catching and chasing the bull which he drags to the cave to slay it.

The focal point of virtually every Mithraic temple (Mithraeum) is an icon showing Mithras slaying the bull. Clearly this represents the central myth of the mysteries. Although the size and shape of the icons and many of the details vary, it is striking how consistently the posture of Mithras is represented. He kneels with his left knee on the bull's back, grasps its nostrils with his left hand, pulling its head back, and stabs it with the dagger in his right hand. His right foot is extended backwards over the bull's right back leg. Since means of mass production were not used the only explanation for this uniformity must be that the details were mythologically or symbolically significant.

Most books interpret the main myth scene in terms of the Zoroastrian myth of creation, except that in Mithraism, it is suggested, it is the god rather than the evil spirit Ahriman who kills the first bull from which creation emerges. The dog and snake are traditional symbols of good and evil so the fact they are shown leaping to the bull's wound has been interpreted as representing the dualistic conflict of good and evil at creation. The scorpion, another Zoroastrian symbol of evil, is shown at the bull's genitals and this is taken as depicting evil seeking to destroy life at its source. But the victory of good over evil, it is said, is indicated by the ears of corn springing from the tail of the moribund victim.

Although this interpretation is found in most books, recent scholarly research has questioned most of it, especially the use of Zoroastrian ideas on good and evil. The motifs of snake and scorpion appear in different contexts in Mithraism, on altars and ritual bowls for example, in such a manner they cannot reasonably be interpreted as symbols of evil. Similarly the motif of a lion often appears on reliefs without any hint that it represents evil to Mithraists, as it did to Zoroastrians. What then do the reliefs represent?

Each of the motifs described corresponds to a constellation in astrological teaching: the bull = Taurus; the dog = Canis Minor or Major; the snake = Hydra; the scorpion = Scorpio and the raven which appears on many reliefs represents Corvus. Other details on the relief also have astrological correspondences: the ears of wheat and the star Spica associated with Virgo; the lion and a large two-handled vase the constellations Leo and Crater. This is too long a list of correspondences for it to be explained by mere coincidence. In the last ten or fifteen years scholars have been forced to reassess their interpretation of Mithraic mythology. Whereas astrology was seen as but a relatively small part of the cult, it is now seen as fundamental to its teaching.

Perhaps the best place to begin an explanation of recent interpretations of Mithraic myths is with a quotation from the third century Neo-Platonic philosopher Porphyry whose account is now thought to be more reliable than had previously been appreciated.

. . . the Persians call the place a cave where they introduce the initiate to the mysteries, revealing to him the path by which souls descend and go back again. For Eubulus [an ancient writer on Mithraism whose works have been lost] tells us that Zoroaster was the first to dedicate a natural cave in honor of Mithras, the creator and father of all; it was located in the mountains near Persia and had flowers and springs. This cave bore for him the image of the cosmos which Mithras had created and the things which the cave contained, by their proportionate arrangement, provided him with symbols of the elements and climates of the cosmos.

De Antro Nympharum 6, Buffalo, 1969

This may be seen as something of the foundation myth of the cult. 'The place where initiates are introduced to the Mysteries' is obviously the temple. Porphyry is, then, saying that Mithraists considered their temple, as 'in the image' of the world cave Mithras had created. This explains why Mithraists used caves as temples where possible, or at least gave temples the internal appearance of a cave or created a sense of being subterranean with steps down to the entrance. The world cave is also shown on many of the reliefs as the setting in which Mithras slew the bull. The temple, therefore, is a physical representation of the sacred space shown on the reliefs, the setting of the myth.

Porphyry also refers to initiates. Quite a lot of information has come down to us regarding Mithraic initiation. From inscriptions and the mosaic aisle of a temple at Ostia we know there were seven grades of initiation, each thought to be under the protection of a planet. In ascending order they were Corax (Raven) under the protection of Mercury; Nymphus (Bride) protected by Venus; Miles (Soldier) protected by Mars; Leo (Lion) protected by Jupiter; Perses (Persian) protected by the moon; Heliodromus (Runner of the Sun) protected by the sun and Pater (Father) under the protection of Saturn. The third-century Christian writer Origen, quoting his contemporary Celsus, wrote of the Mithraic mysteries:

there is a symbol of the two orbits in heaven, the one being that of the fixed stars and the other that assigned to the planets, and of the soul's passage through these. The symbol is this. There is a ladder with seven gates and at its top is an eighth gate.
Contra Celsum VI: 22, Chadwick, p. 334

Putting together the evidence of Porphyry, Origen, certain archaeological sites and recent studies of astrology in Mithraism, it appears that Mithraists believed the human soul descended into the world at birth. The goal of the religious quest was to achieve its ascent out of the world again, involving its passage through seven heavenly gates corre-

These three illustrations show the manner in which Mithraists reproduced features from the myth scene of the cult reliefs on their ritual objects. The ritual vase (*opposite*) in the Römisch-Germanisches Museum, Cologne has the torchbearers either side of the sun god and on the handles are a crouching lion and a coiled snake. The snake handles are clearly illustrated in the pot fragments (*above*) in the Museum Carnuntinum, Bad-Deutsch Altenburg. The vase (*above, top*) in the Hessisches Landesmuseum, Darmstadt, also has snakes on the handle. In addition this has the scorpion from the cult relief (consistently depicted at the bull's genitals, *see* pages 75, 82–3, 86–7) a position indicative of astrological ideas of fertility and the association of zodiacal signs with parts of the body (here Scorpio and genitalia). The three-stepped ladder may be an allusion to the first three grades on the ladder of initiation. This vase recalls that shown underneath the bull on some reliefs (*see* page 78 for example). Just as the cosmic cave of the myth scene was imitated in the physical structure of some temples (*see* the caption on page 83) so, in similar fashion, details from the reliefs were imitated in temple furnishings – and perhaps used in the rituals.

Left The painted Mithraic relief at Marino near Rome. Whereas the Walbrook Mithraeum (page 75) and the Trier Birth scene (page 89) indicate the cosmic cave by a zodiacal circle, at Marino there is a very naturalistic or 'earthly' cave. The panels to the sides of the main scene 'reading' clockwise from bottom left show: Jupiter and the giants; Oceanus; birth of Mithras; Mithras riding the bull; Mithras carrying the bull; Mithras 'anointing' (hitting?) Sol; Mithras and Sol making a treaty and Mithras with bow and arrow. The last six of these are usually interpreted as events in the mythological life of Mithras. Top left of the relief shows the sun shining down on Mithras and top right is the moon - indications of the cosmic dimension of the god's work. This temple is carved deep into a mountainside and is, therefore, one example of a temple made very much as a cave reflecting the cave made by Mithras, the Creator and Father of all.

Above A Mithraeum from Ostia built in the foundations of the Baths of Trajan (mid-second century). It has been argued that, as this is one of the simplest cult statues, it must be one of the first (c.f. pages 78, 82–3). It may be that Mithraism did spread throughout the empire from Rome but we do not know that. The simplicity of the relief is no argument for its priority. The artist may simply have alluded to the main features realising they would trigger known ideas to the worshipper. This is an excellent example of a temple built to resemble a cave. The hole in the roof was precisely located so that the sun's rays fell on the statue at specific times of the year.

There were seven grades of initiation in Mithraism; each stood under the protection of a planetary deity. The progress of the individual through these grades was thought to reflect the ascent of the soul through the heavens. The symbols of the grades shown here are depicted on a mosaic aisle in the Mithraeum of Felicissimus at Ostia.

Clockwise from above left The lowest grade, Raven (*above*) stood under the protection of Mercury represented by the caduceus. The term 'raven' probably relates to the astrological constellation Corax; it may also allude to ideas associated with ravens in contemporary Roman lore (e.g., as the bird of Apollo). The significance of the cup is not known.

The second grade (*above, middle*) is usually termed 'Bride' but that translation is too simple. The word should be nymphe (feminine), but is actually nymphos (masculine). A male bride is a nonsense or a paradox, a fusion of male and female, something beyond human categories. All the terms used of the grades have masculine connotations. Women were excluded from the cult as they were from the army. The diadem (top right) is a sign of the tutelary planet of the grade, Venus. The lamp represents the light brought by the grade, as one Mithraic acclamation expresses it 'Behold Nymphos! Hail Nymphos! Hail New Light!'

The third grade, Soldier *above right* naturally stands under the protection of Mars, and is represented by the helmet and javelin. The third object is generally interpreted as a soldier's kit bag, but it could be the hind leg of the bull with the hoof against the helmet. On some reliefs Mithras is shown swinging such a hind leg apparently hitting Sol on the head –

often loosely described as an 'anointing' scene.

The fourth grade, Lion (*right*), is under the protection of Jupiter (hence the thunderbolt). The fire shovel to the left refers to the role of the grade of burning incense on the altar. In the centre is a sistrum, a 'rattle' used in Egyptian mystery cults, presumably alluding to the Egyptian lore about the mythical roles of lions which were invoked in teaching about the fourth Mithraic grade.

The fifth grade was that of the Persian (*below right*) under the protection of the moon (top right). On entry to the grades of Lion and Persian the initiate was purified with honey. The grade symbols are ears of corn and a sickle for he is said to be 'the keeper of the fruits.'

The sixth grade, Runner of the Sun (*below*), was protected by the Sun and had as his symbols the attributes of Sol; radiate crown, torch and whip.

The highest grade, that of Father (*below, left*) was under the protection of Saturn – whose sickle is represented among the symbols. The Persian cap presumably links with the hat worn by Mithras and the staff portrays authority. The identity of the object on the left is unclear – it may be an eye, or a ring.

(The author is heavily indebted for details in this caption to an article by R. L. Gordon in *Journal of Mithraic Studies*, III, 1980, pp. 19–99.)

One of the most famous painted Mithraic temples, that in the Palazzo Barberini, Rome. Unfortunately the paint is deteriorating, so that older photographs often show more details. Whereas the Walbrook Mithraeum, London (page 75) shows the zodiac as a circle, here it is the shape of the cave roof (as it is on page 78) but which is usually more realistically depicted (see, for example, page 82–3). It is likely that such variations in the art were intended to emphasise different aspects of Mithraic teaching, drawing out, for example, the astrological aspect of the beliefs and at others, perhaps, the emphasis on this world with the naturalistic cave.

sponding to the initiate's ascent through the grades of initiation. Promotion in the cult was, then, seen to correspond to a heavenly journey of the soul. On the side benches of a temple near Naples are a sequence of paintings of a Mithraic initiation. Unfortunately they are badly decayed and do not have any accompanying explanation, so they do not give us a full account. Some of the crucial scenes show the initiate on his knees, naked and bound before one of the grades, presumably a higher one, and then freed. This suggests ideas of submission to religious authority (kneeling); casting off of the old life (nakedness); and liberation from bondage through the mysteries. The epithets applied to the higher grades in inscriptions imply that the path through the grades, and so for the soul through the heavens, was life-long, arduous and ascetic.

For the ascent of the soul the initiate needed a map of the heavens, directions along the path which might be obstructed by certain spiritual powers, but for which he might hope for the aid of other forces. The main cult relief provided just such a map. We no longer understand all the specific details of that map but it is clear that it plots the path along which the sun travels because all the constellations depicted lie either directly along that line (the ecliptic) or are immediately alongside it as pointers to the South. The constellations represented on the reliefs show the passage of the sun from mid-spring (Taurus) through the length of summer (Hydra, Canis Minor and Major, Leo, Crater, Virgo, Corvus) to mid-autumn (Scorpius). The icon is, therefore, in a sense both a map and a calendar. Time and season are represented as well as celestial space. There is also an allegory of the Sun and Moon. Mithras is the sun (in the cult he is called 'the Unconquered Sun God') and the bull, Porphyry states, is the moon (as it appears in astrology). In ancient thought the Sun and Moon were often regarded as both the agents and the points for departure and return of the soul in its descent into the material world and

its reascent when finally liberated. The bull-slaying relief, therefore, depicts not only the route and time of salvation, but also the agencies through which that salvation is realised in birth and celestial rebirth.

There were, almost certainly, different levels of interpretation of the scene according to the degree of spiritual advancement achieved in the grades. At one level, or in one sense, the scene conveyed a teaching of salvation, for an inscription in the Mithraeum under the church of Santa Prisca in Rome refers to Mithras saving men by shedding the eternal blood, presumably that of the bull. Perhaps it was that in some way this was thought to give the elixir of immortality. A scene that is represented on many reliefs is Mithras and Sol sharing a banquet over a table draped with the skin of the bull. On one relief they are attended by some of the grades of initiates which has led scholars to suggest this was a mythical scene enacted by the initiates in the cult, presumably so that they could share in the saving work of the shedding of the blood. Just as the world cave created by Mithras was imitated in the temple building, so the mythical events depicted on the reliefs were made a living force in the rites through imitation. Bowls shown on a number of reliefs both of the bull slaying and the ritual meal, have been copied in bowls found among archaeological remains. Bowls in the myth scene are associated with a lion and a snake, and those found in the temples have a snake or lion shown on them. Both in its structure and its furnishings therefore, the Mithraic temple made mythical places and objects present and effective in the ritual life of the community.

In the 1970s the scholarly study of Roman Mithraism underwent considerable changes. The subject has always been a fascinating academic detective story despite the fact that many of the clues are missing. What we now realise is just how little we know of the Mystery. This account has had to be brief and incomplete. Nothing, for example, has been said about the statues of a human figure, entwined by a snake and with a lion's head. Some have said it represents the Mithraic version of the Zurvan, the High God of Time, others that it represents a variant of the Zoroastrian figure of Ahriman. In the light of recent research it is far more likely that it is concerned with salvation and the soul's celestial ascent. But if scholars do not know whether a statue represents the High God or the devil, all that can really be concluded is that the evidence is unclear. The reader should be warned that what can, at

Clockwise from left
Opposite top One of the most recent Mithraic discoveries (1973–74), a small cult relief, measuring only 3 inches (.075m) across, this was found in a building converted from a warehouse into a Mithraic temple in Caesarea Maritima in Israel. The style of the carving and the structure of the scenes is like that common in the Danubian provinces. Either side of the main act are the torchbearers, Cautes and Cautopates, who with their raised and lowered torches symbolise both the rising and setting sun (in its daily and the seasonal movements) and the ascending and descending of the soul out of and into birth. Above are the sun and moon; then below, left to right, Mithras laying his hand on Sol – the ritual meal and Mithras riding the bull.

Below A Mithraic ritual meal scene dated *c.* A.D. 140 discovered at Ladenburgh by Dr. B. Heükemes in 1965. This relief, together with the associated finds, will be published when permission has been granted to complete excavations of the surrounding land and the Mithraeum. The relief (height 4.6 ft or 1.40m., width 5ft or 1.50m., depth 1ft. or 0.30m.), was originally painted. The author is heavily indebted to Dr. Heükemes for being allowed to publish the first picture of this significant relief. The scene shows Mithras and Sol with drinking cups reclining on a couch draped with a bull skin behind a table with bulls' legs on which fruit is set. The stylised arch appears to represent a cave.

Opposite, bottom An 'ordeal pit' at the rear of the Carrawburgh Mithraeum near Newcastle upon Tyne. Such coffin-shaped pits have occasionally been found in other Mithraea. It has been suggested that they were used as places for testing the initiate and that there was something of the idea of dying to the old life and rising to the new at initiation.

Opposite second from bottom This scene of Mithras' birth from the rock is typical of many such scenes showing him as a naked youth (not a baby), with Phrygian cap and holding a symbol (orb) of sovereignty. It is unusual but important because it probably makes links explicit which elsewhere are only implied: the circular zodiac represents the cosmic cave (see page 75); the dog, snake and raven link with the main bull-slaying scene and the lion, vase and thunderbolt are symbols of the lion-headed figure (page 90). Interpreting iconographic' symbols without any explanatory text is problematic with any religion, nowhere more so than with Mithraism. Rheinisches Landesmuseum, Trier.

first sight, appear to be a factual re-telling of a myth can in fact be a tendentious interpretation or even sheer guess work!

But whatever the problems of reconstructing Roman Mithraic mythology, Mithra remains a god whose worship spans many centuries and continents: in ancient and modern India, in ancient Iran and living Zoroastrianism, as well as, for some three hundred years, in the Roman Empire. The god of Truth and Order, the enemy of the Lie, the destroyer of Falsehood, the creator and father of all, the one who saves men, has been the focus of a rich and divergent mythology for some 4,000 years.

Left, top This is perhaps the most famous relief relating to the Mithraic ritual meal. Many reliefs show Mithras and Sol sharing a 'banquet', denoted by grapes, wine and bread (*see* pages 88–9) over the bull's body or a table draped with its skin. The distinctive feature of this monument is that it shows some of the grades sharing the banquet. From left to right the Raven (note the mask); Bride (or Persian); 'Runner of the Sun'; Father (these two in place of Sol and Mithras?); Persian (or Bride); and, Lion (note the mask). This appears to omit Soldier and leaves the lion near the table unexplained. Some have suggested this depicts events in Mithraic rites literally, hence that Mithraists wore masks in the rites; or often, more plausibly, that it depicts the mythical 'first time' when they believed the rite was performed, when the mythical prototypes of the grades attended the gods, which myth was re-enacted in the cult. Zemaljski Muzej, Sarajevo.

Left, bottom This is commonly referred to as the lion-headed figure. It is often shown encircled by a snake (here winding from the lower right leg round the torso with its head protruding through the mane on the lion head). Many statues also show the figure with wings. On this monument the figure is holding a fire shovel like that used by the grade of Lion (see page 85). One recent suggestion has, therefore, been that this represents a mythological being associated with that grade. Museum für Vor-und Frühgeschichte, Frankfurt.

Opposite Head of Mithras from the Walbrook Mithraeum, London. The Museum of London.

Myth and the Prophet

Zoroaster was a historical figure, a man born at a particular place at a particular time, even though we do not know for certain where or when. His hymns, the *Gathas*, are personal compositions with the clear ring of authenticity. The rise of Zoroastrianism cannot be understood without accepting the existence of such a person. The purpose of this chapter is not to undermine the historicity of the figure, but to see how, as with all religions, the stories of the founder's work have been adapted and developed by his followers. The faithful have a need to visualise the founder clearly 'and have therefore unconsciously added to the accounts handed down to them the details that did this for them. It will be well if the reader says to himself: "Here is the story that millions have taken for truth, *and they have also lived by it; but* the historians are very doubtful of its accuracy" ' (Noss, p. 156, n). In trying to understand what a prophet means to his followers the developed myth or legend can be of greater help than a purely scholarly reconstruction of history.

For the Greeks Zoroaster was the archetypal magus or priest, the great Persian sage. Plato is said to have wanted to travel to the Orient and learn from his 'pupils', the magi. There is even a tradition that Socrates had a magus for a teacher. Many famous Greeks, including Aristotle, knew the Persian teachings, and a number of books apparently circulated throughout the Greek world under the name of Zoroaster. The Greeks placed Zoroaster in hoary antiquity, dating him six thousand years before Plato, an adaptation and misunderstanding of the Zoroastrian scheme of history. Such awe for the ancient oriental sage must, of course, derive ultimately from the Persian attitude to the prophet, but this is not mythology; for that we have to look at the beliefs surrounding the life of the teacher of the Good Religion.

The coming of Zoroaster, it is believed, was foretold to a number of holy beings. It was first told to the primeval ox who had been slain by Ahriman when he first attacked the world. The soul of the ox protested to the creator that it had no protector in the world of creatures. When it was shown that the heavenly self, or *fravashi*, of Zoroaster would come to protect the species, then the ox was satisfied and consented to return to earth to nourish mankind. The coming of Zoroaster was also foretold to Yima in the paradisal age. A patriarchal king, the prince Us, was told of the coming of Zoroaster by the ox and in one of the ancient *Yashts* it is said that the Divine Glory had been passed from saint to saint so that it could illumine the soul of Zoroaster. Thus Zoroaster, to the Zoroastrian, is no historical accident. Not only is he the turning point of history, his birth marking the beginning of the millennium when evil would be defeated, but he is also the *foreordained* turning point of history to which creation has looked since Ahriman first attacked the world.

A bull-headed column from the palace of Persepolis. It has been suggested that these motifs were not simply decorative, but rather symbols of the mighty power of the king and the fertility of his domains. The style and decorative motifs became models for much later Persian art and architecture.

Zoroaster was not conceived in the ordinary way. Three parts of his being passed through the heavens to earth where they were united in the body of Dughdov, a girl of fifteen – the ideal age in Persian thought. His 'heaven sent glory' (*khwarr*) came from the world of light via sun, moon and stars to the hearth of Dughdov's father where it started a perpetually burning fire. The glory then passed into the body of Dughdov's mother and thence into Dughdov herself while she was still in the womb. When she was born with this glory, light radiated from her. Demons, ever ready to defile good, spread the word in people's minds that her radiance showed her to be a sorceress and her father sent her away. But in her new home she met Pourushasp, her husband and Zoroaster's father, so that, as often happens, the forces of light turned the work of evil to good.

The second part of Zoroaster's being to pass from the heavens was his *fravahr*, or guardian spirit. It was brought from the place where the Bounteous Immortals dwell by the divine messenger, Neryosang, and the ideal king of yore, Yima. It was set in the stem of the haoma plant and placed on the top of a tall tree. While walking near the tree, the young married couple, Pourushasp and Dughdov, saw the plant and with the help of the Bounteous Immortals Pourushasp reached it and bore it to

his bride. So it was that the heavenly beings brought the heavenly spirit of the prophet to earth ready to do battle with evil.

The third part of Zoroaster to be borne to earth was his physical body, the *tan-gohr*. The Bounteous Immortals responsible for water and plants, Haurvatat and Ameretat, caused warm rains to fall for man and cattle. Guided by the other Immortals, Pourushasp led heifers out to graze and though they had never had calves the rain-nourished grass produced milk in their udders. This milk mixed with the juice from the haoma plant produced Zoroaster's body in Dughdov's womb. The glory, the spirit and the body of the prophet thus united through the aid of heavenly powers to bring to birth the divinely sent prophet who would conquer evil.

At the birth of Zoroaster all the creatures of the Good Creation, the plants and the waters, rejoiced, but the demons were terror-struck. They knew that where the gods had failed to smite them, Zoroaster could. The birth of the prophet was an answer to the prayers and offerings of haoma by his father; it was also a remarkable birth. As soon as he was brought forth he laughed, a light shone around the house, and, most significant of all, from the moment of birth he was able to converse with Ohrmazd. Conscious of his mission from the first, Zoroaster declared

himself a worshipper of Ohrmazd.

Like so many of the great religious teachers Zoroaster is believed to have been the object of continued demonic attempts to destroy or seduce him from the right path. Having failed before his birth, they now sought to kill him in infancy. They led Pourushasp to believe that Zoroaster's radiant glory was due to the presence of evil, so the father tried to kill his own son. First he laid Zoroaster on firewood and tried to set fire to it – but the fire would not blaze and burn the baby. Then he laid the child in the path of a stampeding herd of oxen, but the leading ox stood protective guard over him until all was safe. A similar attempt, and rescue, was made with stampeding horses. Then the baby was put in the lair of a she-wolf whose young had been taken away, but instead of attacking the infant she protected him. There were, thus, numerous attempts to destroy the prophet. True to its nature evil sought to destroy the good. But even the most deadly assaults of the forces of darkness can be overcome by the righteous. These efforts continued by

The wondrous life of Zoroaster, especially his miraculous protection from evil – both from stampeding cattle and from burning – continues to be a popular feature of living Zoroastrianism. A conviction of Zoroastrians throughout the ages, in all continents and in the various forms of the faith, is that Zoroaster had a personal vision of God.

These pictures are taken from a popular little book written for the laity by the high priest K. S. Dabu, *Zarathushtra and His Teachings*, Union Press, Bombay, 1962. These and many other modern Parsi paintings are more influenced by Western Sunday-School art than by traditional Iranian or Indian styles.

means of sorcery, treachery and dispute as the prophet grew up, but all were in vain, foiled either by divine intervention or because the young Zoroaster was able to confound the teachings of the elders. A series of stories are told illustrating the compassion of the prophet for animals – displaying thereby an important Zoroastrian virtue.

As the prophet grew up he displayed the wisdom, devotion and discrimination which were to characterize his later mission. On one occasion a priest who reverenced false gods was visiting the child's home and was invited by the parents to recite prayers before the meal. Zoroaster in his youth, as in adulthood, was totally opposed to false religion and protested vigorously. The priest condemned the young prophet, and was struck dead as he left the house. Evil should be condemned wherever it is found, and its worst threats can be overcome by the power of the good.

Although functioning as a priest Zoroaster also spent time in a desert cave, pursuing his religion in solitude and meditating in silence for years before he had his first vision at the age of thirty. One day as he was fetching pure water from a river for the haoma pressing, he had a premonition of the vision which was to be given him. Then before him he saw a transcendent figure of enormous proportions. After laying aside his body he was transported into the presence of the angels, where he took a seat among the enquirers in heaven and was instructed in the Good Religion. This was the first of eight visions Zoroaster had of God and his Good Mind. Thus through Zoroaster there is a direct communication to man of the Truth from heaven. Zoroaster through his personal experience of God was able to reveal to man the will of the divine.

His teaching was rejected at first. Men were hard of heart and Zoroaster needed the comfort of God. After the period of visions was over and the revelation complete, he was tempted by the demons, who sought to destroy him, to persuade him to worship them and to destroy the faith with false visions. But all was in vain. Zoroaster was resolute in the faith, steadfast in the recital of the sacred prayers and faithful in his practice of the Zoroastrian rituals. He stands as the true model and guide for all his followers in the trials and temptations that beset them.

As in most religious traditions, the Zoroastrians believe that the hand of God was at work in the ministry of the great prophet, particularly in the early conversions. Followers are drawn by the manifestations of God in the miraculous work of the teacher. When Zoroaster had made his first converts, guided by God, he visited the palace of the king, Vishtaspa, that he might convert him also. The royal court was a home of superstition, magic and suspicion. The learned men of the court disputed with Zoroaster for three whole days, but as the prophet's ability to know the king's thoughts was impressing Vishtaspa, the wicked and jealous priests hatched a plot against him and Zoroaster was cast into prison as a necromancer. Then a miracle occurred: the king's favourite black horse grew ill and its legs drew up into its body so that it could not move. Zoroaster offered to restore the horse to its full health on the granting of four conditions. The first was that the king should accept the faith; the second was that the warlike prince, Isfandiyar, should fight for the Good Religion; the third was that the queen should accept the Good Religion, and the fourth was that the names of the plotters must be revealed. As each condition was granted one of the horse's legs was restored until the horse returned to perfect health and vigour.

After his conversion Vishtaspa asked that he might know his place in heaven, whereupon three archangels appeared at the monarch's court. Their glory filled the palace so that the king and his courtiers trembled, but their fears were calmed for the protective presence of God at court was promised and victory over their foes assured. The king was granted his petition for a vision of his place in heaven, and his son, Peshyotan, was given immortality. Isfandiyar was made invulnerable in the defence of the Good Religion, and the Grand Vizier was given universal wisdom. The court was thus converted and the victorious march of the Zoroastrian faith began. With the aid of God the Good Religion was given the support of an earthly king, the heavenly teaching became available to men and the miraculous powers of the prophet were made manifest.

Naturally, legends have grown up about the king, the court and Zoroaster's later life and about missionary work in distant lands. But these clearly belong to the category of legend and indicate little of the position of the prophet in the mythology of Zoroastrianism, unlike the birth, vision and conversion narratives, which through their religious significance can be classed as myth.

Regarding the death of Zoroaster the Persian tradition is unanimous in attributing it to the hand of a murderer. Aged seventy-seven, the prophet was killed while in the sanctuary. The Persian sources give few details and there is nothing suggestive of myth or legend about them. A mythical form is, however, given by Christian writers. This represents a deliberate attempt to bring Zoroaster into disrepute, and provides a good example of the way in which myth can be used to bring discredit to an opponent. The source behind the many versions which exist seems to be the Clementine *Recognitions*. Zoroaster is identified with Ham, the son of Noah, and to deceive people he used to conjure up the stars until a presiding genie, angry at his control, destroyed Zoroaster, the arch-

magician, with fire from heaven. The Persians, ever fools, deified the ashes and praised the star which they claimed transported Zoroaster into the presence of God. This is said to explain the form of his name, 'Zoro' is taken as the Greek for life, 'aster' the Greek for star, hence 'the living star'. The early Christians, in common with many religious traditions, were quite good at 'mud-slinging'.

From various sources we have been able to reconstruct something of the mythical development of the figure of Zoroaster. The dating of this development is very difficult, and for present purposes totally unnecessary. These myths show how the historical figure of Zoroaster was understood by the faithful, and what he meant to them as their great religious teacher. He is their ideal man, the one who revealed the will of God to man, the one who communicated with God, the one who wrought fear in the hearts of evil forces and who, on the human scale, is chiefly responsible for their destruction. In these myths one can see the projection of the great cosmic battles into the life of the person who may be called the archetypal Zoroastrian. The fact that he is the authority for many of their rituals should not be interpreted, as it has been by some scholars, as evidence that he is a cultic creation. This is a natural religious tendency, just as Christians trace the history of the Eucharist back to the life and actions of Jesus. As the first Zoroastrian priest and missionary it is inevitable that Zoroaster should be viewed as the inspiration of the Zoroastrian religious life. Equally natural is the idea that all three social classes, priest, warrior and husbandman, should be contained in his being, for what great saviour could neglect a major body of society? Some have asked whether Zoroaster is though of as a god or man in the myths. This is an unnecessary question. Although he is said to be more effective than all the *Yazatas* in defeating evil, this is only because Ohrmazd has chosen him as the vessel to bear the Good Religion into the world. Zoroaster is often presented talking to Ohrmazd and the faithful revere the great teacher, but Zoroaster forever remains man, Ohrmazd the sovereign Lord.

Myth and the King

In the ancient Near East the king was often thought of as divine and his person and function were surrounded by myth. In this section we shall look at Persian belief to see if a similar pattern presents itself there.

In these days of central heating and refrigeration it is difficult for many of us to understand the ancient sense of complete dependence on the regularity of the seasons. In Egypt the sequence of the seasons was quite regular, but this was far from being so in Mesopotamia. There life was insecure and men believed that unless they could participate in the cosmic events survival could not be guaranteed. A mediator between man and the gods was needed and, they believed, supplied in the person of the king.

It is well known that the ancient Egyptians believed the king to be divine, the son of Re, the source of stability and security. In Mesopotamia there was a similar idea, but with important differences. There the king was not the physical offspring of the gods, but on the day of his accession to the throne he became the adopted son of god and he henceforth acted as god on earth and represented the people before the gods. One of his primary tasks was to ensure the proper sequence of the seasons so that his flock might live. The ordering of the seasons was achieved through an annual ritual, the New Year Festival, in which the king, taking the part of the god, re-enacted the primeval battle whereby god had defeated the forces of chaos in the shape of a monster, and had produced order in the world. This drama was not just a symbol of what *had* happened, it was also an effective source which ensured that the same creative order would be released in the coming year so that life would again triumph over the forces of chaos.

Persia bordered on Mesopotamia and had many close contacts with her; how far did the Persians take over this belief and practice?

In Persian thought there are two instruments of the forces of good in their combat with evil, the brothers of religion and kingship. The two co-exist but do not coincide. Obedience to the king and knowledge of the Good Religion are the two factors necessary to the defeat of evil. In an ideal state 'Religion is royalty, and royalty is Religion' (Dk. M. 47:6, ZDT, p. 296). Anarchy is, fundamentally, a product of evil religion. The good king manifests the Bounteous Spirit of God and is a symbol of his sovereignty on earth. It is his duty to expand the creation, the Good Religion and the happiness of his subjects, for these are the manifestations of God's desires for mankind. Although the Good Religion was first propounded in Persia, it is essentially a message for all mankind.

In Persian mythology the ideal king was thought to be Yima, and *Nauruz*, the festival instigated by Yima, is the Persian New Year Festival. In the Sasanian period kings were definitely thought of as divine; they were said to be the brothers of the sun and moon and were called gods. On a number of reliefs it is Ohrmazd himself who invests them with the insignia of kingship and their crowns bear the symbols of the different gods. The supernatural character of the kings is indicated on a number of reliefs by the presence of a halo, the Divine Glory. The great king Khusrau

depicted himself enthroned in heaven surrounded by the stars. Thus there is little doubt of the divine character of the Sasanian kings.

What of the earlier period and what mythological significance and functions were attached to this position? Here the question is much more difficult to answer, but in view of the contact of Persia with other nations and the deployment of foreign labour it would be surprising

if some influence were not felt. When Cyrus the Great (559-530 B.C.) ruled Babylonia he had his son, Cambyses, installed as king of Mesopotamia according to the traditional Babylonian manner at the New Year Festival in 538. Cyrus wished to make his son acceptable to the Babylonians by having him installed with a ceremony of approval and adoption by their god Marduk. The same prince was presented in Egypt as son

Ardashir II (A.D. 379–383) is shown receiving the crown from Ohrmazd (on the right). On the left is Mithra with a crown composed of the rays of the sun, holding the sacred barsom and standing on a lotus plant, a sacred symbol. While Mithra appears in a priestly role, Ardashir II and Ohrmazd stand like conquering heroes on the body of a vanquished enemy. A relief from Taq-i Bustan.

Above A cylinder seal impression of Darius. The inscription records his name in old Persian, Elamite and Babylonian. The king, under the protection of Ahura Mazda, does battle with raging lions. One lion rising on his hind legs like a demonic being recalls the style of the ancient Assyrians and those cultures on the Iranian borders influenced by them (*see* page 23). In a seal used for international trade it is reasonable that such scripts and styles were used. Nevertheless one wonders whether some of the ancient Near Eastern ideas of kingship were also taken over. British Museum, London.

Opposite A relief from Naqsh-i Rustam of the third or fourth century A.D. showing the goddess Anahita (on the right) investing the king Narseh with the symbol of kingship. The very ornate style used on this relief can also be seen on a number of Sasanian coins. The rippling effect on the goddess' clothes may be intended to recall her character as goddess of the waters.

of the Egyptian god Re. Naturally one wonders if these actions reflected or influenced the Persian idea of kingship.

Cambyses is not the only figure for whom we have suggestions of the idea of sacred kingship. Darius (522-486 B.C.) was largely responsible for the construction of a magnificent palace at Persepolis in south-west Persia. The size, beauty and magnificence of this city is hard to describe. Covering an enormous area, huge buildings were erected with a wealth of detailed reliefs and carvings, a work which we know took many years. Yet the palace was rarely used. Among the remains there is little or nothing to suggest that it was ever used for administrative purposes. Persepolis appears rather as a ritual centre, the scene of the annual festival where the peoples of the empire gathered to pay their dues and tokens of loyalty to the king of kings. Processions passed up a staircase so constructed that a horse could be ridden up it, through gate-houses into a hall of a hundred columns — which, it has been suggested, resembled the sacred grove — past crenellated walls symbolising the sacred mountain. These processions were not merely displays of wealth but displays before God of the fruitfulness of the land. The *Nauruz* festival has connections with the seasons, for it coincides

Right The exterior of Darius' palace at Susa was decorated with multi-coloured glazed bricks, giving a wonderfully delicate effect. This scene shows a pair of winged genii beneath the winged symbol of Ahura Mazda. It is yet another example of motifs taken over from Babylon.

Opposite top On this rock relief from Naqsh-i Rustam Ohrmazd (right) offers the diadem and gift of kingship to Ardashir I (A.D. 224–241). The king is not presented as smaller than the god, nor as bending the knee before him; indeed his crown stands higher than that of Ohrmazd. Just as Ohrmazd tramples on the head of the devil, Ahriman, so Ardashir tramples on Ardavan, the last Parthian king. Ohrmazd is shown holding the barsom, the symbol of his priestly person.

Opposite, bottom Note the detail of the snake in the devil's headdress, seen in the illustration above under the raised foot, of Ohrmazd's horse, the one on the right

with the feast of Rapithwin (see p. 30), the time when prayer is offered for the return of the god from his hiding place in the earth where he has kept alive plant roots despite winter's onslaughts. The battle of the seasons may be symbolised in some reliefs which show a lion (the sun) slaying a bull (the rains). The reliefs at Persepolis suggest that there was an annual festival in Persia which was associated with the struggle of the seasons and forces of life.

The king's role in all this is not clear. In their many inscriptions the kings present themselves as completely dependent on Ahura Mazda. It is Ahura Mazda who makes them king, who gives them strength, who protects them, their lands and all they do. But it is the kings who make effective the will of god on earth. Darius in an inscription at Susa proclaims that he copies the work of God for he, like God, makes the world excellent (*frasha*):

By the grace of Ahura Mazda I have done this, that which I have done appears frasha *to the whole world.*
Kent, p. 141

On the reliefs the kings are represented under the hovering winged symbol of Ahura Mazda, fairly clear signs that they represent God on earth. Did they take part in a ritual battle with the powers of evil as in Babylonia? We do not know. There are a number of reliefs and seals on which the king is shown fighting with a monster. The style of the seals suggests Babylonian influence and again one wonders if it was only the outward art form which was taken over.

In later times at least then, the Persian king was thought of as divine. He was the essential complement to the priest, for religion and kingship are brothers. His archetype was Yima, the primeval king who ruled in peace, expanded the world, but fought no battles. If the ancient Persians took over anything of the Babylonian concept of the king it does not appear that they thought of him as the son of God, but rather as God's special representative, working under his protection. He was himself so exalted that his face was masked before the people, his presence concealed behind a curtain and ordinary

Above The motif of a lion attacking a bull occurs twenty-seven times at Persepolis and thereafter in much Persian art. Its frequent appearance and key locations (near the throne room) at Persepolis strongly suggest it had important symbolic significance, but we do not know precisely what that was. One interpretation is that the creatures represent the astrological signs of Leo and Taurus and the sequence of the seasons. As a lion is a symbol of kingship, it may also express the mighty power of the monarch which devours all enemies.

Opposite There are doorways on all four walls of the throne room at Persepolis. In the door jambs the king is shown as a hero overcoming wild beasts. In this particular scene the emphasis is on the cosmic nature of the beast – a lion with wings, a scorpion's tail and claw feet. The posture of hero and monster resembles that in Near Eastern art (see page 23).

Opposite The Sasanian monarch Khusrau II (A.D. 591–628) carved an arched cave out of rock in a hunting park by a stream issuing from the mountain at Taq-i Bustan. Over the arch Roman-style victories bring the ring of sovereignty. *Left* At the back of the cave the king (centre) is shown receiving the diadem from Ohrmazd (right) while Anahita also offers a diadem (left). Beneath the investiture the king is shown as a knight on horseback in full armour. On the side walls of the cave the king is shown hunting: on the right hunting deer, and boars on the other side, a relief shown *below*. The elephant riders on the left drive the boar into the swamps on which the king sails. In the centre the king is shown shooting boar and on the right the boar is seen dead and the monarch comes safely to dry land. The movement of animals from left to right carries the eye from one scene to the next. The king's importance is stressed by his size and domination of the centre relief, but also by the 'halo' which surrounds his head, symbolising the presence of the divine glory, or *hvarenah*.

men prostrated themselves before him. Perhaps to the ordinary people the great king of kings was more than man and the masses may even in early times have seen in him the present manifestation of the legendary kings who slew dragons and ruled over demons. To the king and the priests the royal role was to overcome the disruptive forces at work within the empire. When rebels arose, to use the words of the great Darius himself, it was 'the Lie that made them rebellious'. The great cosmic battle between the Truth and the Lie was a battle in which the king was engaged, but the emphasis seems to have been on his role in establishing the order and peace of God's kingdom in his own realm with the aid of the Wise Lord rather than on a ritual ordering of the seasons, though the one need not exclude the other. The Persians could not have been unaware of the Babylonian myths of kingship, but they appear to have transferred myth into history and in their mythical symbols expressed their conviction that the good king manifests the Bounteous Spirit of God. They looked for the day when perfect kingship would combine with the Good Religion, for then the renovation would occur.

Above The Cyrus cylinder from Babylon is a contemporary record by Cyrus of his policy towards subject peoples after his capture of Nineveh. He ordered the restoration of temples and deported peoples. It was as a result of this edict that the faithful of the Jewish exiles in Babylon returned to Israel and began to rebuild the temple. British Museum, London.

Opposite The crowns worn by the Sasanian kings embodied the symbols of different gods. The battlements on those of Shapur I and II may be derived from Achaemenid styles; the rays on the crown of Bahram I are from the symbol for Mithra; the leaves on Narseh's crown have been ascribed to Anahita; the wings and eagle's head on the crown of Hohrmizd II may symbolise Verethraghna, the god of victory. Peroz I, Khusrau II and Yezdegerd III employed the symbol of the Moon god, Mah. The royal crown was so heavy that it could not rest on the king's head but was suspended from the ceiling over the throne.

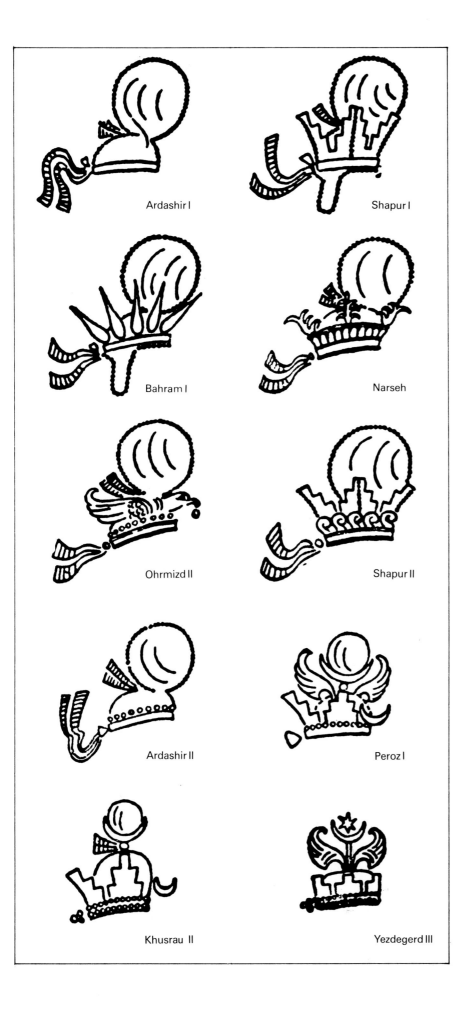

Ardashir I

Shapur I

Bahram I

Narseh

Ohrmizd II

Shapur II

Ardashir II

Peroz I

Khusrau II

Yezdegerd III

Myth and History

Myth as an Interpretation of History
In one sense all myth is part of history, for myth embodies the views of man about himself, his world and its development. This is particularly true of the myths of the Persians, for their myths of creation and the renovation are interpretations of, or reflections upon, the process of world history. As we have seen they divided world history into four periods, each of three thousand years. The first two periods are concerned with creation, the third is the period when the wills of Ohrmazd and Ahriman are mixed in the world, and the fourth period is the time when evil will be overcome. The first thousand years of the last period are divided into ages of gold, silver, steel and iron, the last age being a time when evil will assault the world with renewed vigour. The purpose of this myth is to explain how God's good world can be so full of evil, darkness, pain, suffering and death. The answer is that history is the battleground between God and all that is good and the devil and all that is evil.

But the purpose of the myth is not only to interpret the past; it also explains the present in such a way that men may hope for, and trust in, the future. With the fall of the Sasanian empire the Zoroastrian religion faced enormous problems. It was not simply that there were mass conversions to Islam – caused either by sincerity, the hope of gain, or fear. The problem lay much deeper than that. According to the traditional myth the first saviour was expected one thousand years after Zoroaster. With Zoroaster's dates given in Pahlavi texts that meant the saviour should have come about the year A.D

400. But in the seventh century the Persian empire collapsed and with it, it seemed, the religion. There was a crisis of faith. Was it that God had deserted them? Was it that their whole religion was false? The writers of the Pahlavi books try to answer these questions; they seek to reconcile myth and history.

There are two ways in which the Pahlavi writers tackle the burning question of their day. One text, the *Bahman Yasht*, accounts for the delay in the coming of the saviour by inserting three additional periods into the traditional four which precede his coming. To the ages symbolised by gold, silver, steel and iron are added, after the age of steel, those of brass, copper and lead. Although this answered the question of why the saviour had not come – with the answer that he was still not due – it did not answer the deeper question of whether God had failed in the hour of need, the time of the Islamic invasion. It is to this question that the compilers of the *Bundahishn* and the *Denkard* address themselves in certain chapters. The ancient Avestan scheme of history taught that the age of iron would be a period of distress, when the religion would decline, social and family life would disintegrate and disorder would be rampant everywhere, not just on earth, but in the cosmos also, in the form of drought and pestilence. The Pahlavi writers see in the invasion of Persia the fulfilment or working out of this scheme. The invaders are called 'demons' and they are the brood of the demons of greed. They break up families, causing harm and distress. To the compilers the invaders represented the outbreak of

ركشاهان بافزو فرهنگوری	كتاكرد بنياد كيتی خدای	ذكرفتار دهقان جبين كردياد	سورخ كه تاريخ عالم نهاد
بداخت برمرد دهقان خراج	جونشستن رختی بهادتاج	سرنامداران كيومرث بود	نخستين خدبوی كه كشوركشود

جهانرا ببنامی نكوعهد كرد راويان آمارمرآزان بادشاه بكامكارا اخبارجبين كرده آند مداد وهش خلق را وعده كرد
كيومرث از أسباط مهلائيل بود وزجر الأنساب فرهنگ بدصلی آدم نشته است وامام حجة الأسلام محمدبن محمدبن الغزالی رحه
دركتاب نصيحة الملوك آورده است كه كيومرث برادر زيثث بود وبعضی كويند ازاولادنوح است ودررغم طايفه أزمغان
كيومرث خود مرآست علی الجمله أختلاف أنساب انفاق ازنكه نخستين بادشاهی ست ازبادشاهان جهان ومعنی كيومرث
بلغت سريانی حی ناطق ست يعنی زنده كويا وحقيقت اسم او بامستمی مطابقی دارد بادوجود بسطت ملك وكثرت سباه ووقاد
امر مشعوف بود بسياحت ومازل ومرأجل رخت قدم آوردن وشها كرد كوه ودشت كشتن وبحرار وسواحل كذشتن
وجوزان تدبير ملك ومصالح رعيت بيرد راختی دررشعان مهاوی مهيب وشعاب شواخ عطيم ماوا ساختی وشبها وروزها
سبوجه وعبادت كله انبدی جون زقاب كرد نكشانی دررقه عهد ويمان وطوق عمود وفومان آوردبا ديوان ومرد وعفاريت شياطين محاربات
وسلاح اوجوب وفلاختی بود ولباس اوازبوست كوينده دبوربنی آدم شكا زده راوندنده ملكشا كرده

ودوستی ودشمنی وحرب بادديوان ظامربودی تابوقت نوح بعد ازطوفا بر خلق نا بديدشدند ودرايام كيومرث لباس آدميان ازجلود
حيوانات بود ومردمان ازديوان در رحمت بودند او خلابوبر ازظلم أيشان خلاص داد وديوانرا ازايبا براندند وجناح عدل
واحسان برسرأنی آدمكبرد ودركشف ظلام ظلمان وقضا حواتج مظلو فان مال نعمودو كفت أن ملك لأرض ابمرالله
منزبادشاه زمين ونكاه دارد جرم خلقام نفرهان خدأی تعالی ولقب اوكشاه بود نزد نشستن كاه خود نزد بلك دماوندساخت
وبغايت خوبصورت بود وباقر اورادو فرزند آمدمشی ومشانه نام نهاد مشی منكره مونث ومشانه كويد بعضی كوبد مشك
أول فرزنداوست ومشی بنيات زاهد ومتعبد بود روزی ازلهم برسيد كه أزكاره حه بهتر زبد شركت كرازاری
مردمان وبرستش خدأی عزوجل مشك هميش آزری شوان بود مكرخدابودن ازأيشان وطاعت نتوان كرد كردن ها وبدين
سيب ازخلابوكرانه كرفت ودركوه نبری بردروقتی او وقتی او مشی بدربديدبكا می وبدين او بدبر آمدبكا می بس كروبی ازآن

demonic forces expected in the last century of the millennium. The writer of one text, therefore, looked for signs of the cosmic disorder that he believed must accompany this onslaught. Seeing no such obvious signs he warned that they must be happening in secret.

pestilence is secretly advancing and deceiving so that deaths become more numerous
Dk. VII, 8, 19

Thus the *Bundahishn* and the *Denkard*, despite their initial appearance of being dry academic collections of ancient myths, are in fact powerful appeals and messages of comfort to the faithful. They are preaching the message that the terror which many face, the threat to life and home, is not unforeseen or beyond the power of God to overcome. The faith, the message runs, is not in vain. Men must hold fast and take heart, for this is the fulfilment of the millennium. Soon a prince will come who will restore Iran; the saviour will be born; God will overthrow the devil and the demons.

Although these texts are compilations of ancient material, this material was adapted to meet the spiritual needs of Zoroastrians in a specific situation. Their interpretations of traditional myths in the light of contemporary history provide a stake for the faithful.

Reconstructing History from Myth
The ancient myths of the dragon-slaying heroes were adapted to history in a totally different way from the prophetic adaptation of the myths concerning the end of the world. The later Persian texts and early Muslim historians used the myths of Gayomart, Yima and the rest as a base for a legendary history of Persia from the day of creation to the time of the Islamic invasion. This use of myth is perhaps more interesting for the poetic form given to the history by Firdausi in the *Shah name*, but even in this work much of the spirit of the ancient dualism is retained. The following outline is based almost entirely on the *Shah name*.

Gayomart, the first man of the Zoroastrian myth of creation, appears as the first king who ruled over the whole world. His home was in the mountains and he is pictured wearing leopard skins. Clothing and food were discovered by him and he was reverenced by all, a reverence which gave rise to religion. His rule, which lasted for thirty years, was as benevolent as the sun while Gayomart himself was great in majesty. Hoshang was the grandson of Gayomart. He was entrusted with the task of exacting vengeance on the black demon for the murder of his father. Hoshang's army consisted of

wild and tame animals, birds and supernatural beings, and with it he routed the army of the black demon and cut the villain's head off. With this victory achieved, the aged Gayomart was able to die in peace and victorious Hoshang assumed his throne of splendour. Three gifts arose from his reign: the use of metal, farming and fire. Regarding the last, the *Shah name* reports that as Hoshang was out riding one day he was confronted by a most strange creature:

In its head were two eyes like pools of blood and from its mouth there poured black smoke covering the earth with gloom.
Levy, p. 7

Hoshang threw a stone at the creature. The stone hit another stone and produced a spark; the creature was destroyed; and fire was born. Hoshang's son, Takhmoruw, reigned for thirty years, in which time he subjugated the demons so that he was able to pass on to his son Yima (Jamshid in the *Shah name*) a world of peace.

Jamshid organised mankind into the various social classes. He set apart priests, established the warrior class, deputed some to be husbandmen and others to be concerned with the various crafts. He himself was both king and priest and introduced a number of beneficial products into the world: diverse crafts, medicines and precious jewels. In his reign all was peace and plenty; the demons were made to toil; men didn't work; no one died. Jamshid made a throne; the demons lifted it so that

he sat upon that throne like the sun in the firmament. To celebrate, that day was called a new day – the festival of Now-ruz – the first day of the year.
Levy, p. 10

Left The evil Zahhak seated on his throne. The Evil One implanted snakes on the tyrant's shoulders (snakes are considered evil In Zoroastrianism, *see* page 56), and these needed human brains for their daily food. A characteristic feature of the rule of a wicked king is that people die needlessly. Metropolitan Museum of Art, New York. Gift of Alexander Smith Cochran, 1913.

Opposite The wicked Zahhak was finally defeated – as all evil will be in Persian mythology. In this scene Zahhak (the snakes still shown on his shoulders) is led bound by chains before the triumphant hero, Faridun. Bibliothèque Nationale, Paris.

But Jamshid became conceited, he recited his achievements and declared that men should entitle him creator of the world. At this men deserted his court and his glory disappeared. The future appeared black.

The story is now transferred to the court of a much respected prince, Merdas. Merdas had a brave and active son, Zahhak. One day the devil appeared at the court in the guise of a visitor and beguiled Zahhak with his talk. The innocent youth swore an oath never to divulge the words of the devil and to obey his commands. The devil, tempting the youth with visions of regal power, persuaded him to kill his father and take the throne.

The devil then appeared to Zahhak in the form of a cook and led him astray by giving him meat to eat. Until this time men had been vegetarians. The devil asked that he might kiss the shoulders of so great a monarch, beguiling the youth with flattery. When he had done so the devil disappeared into the ground and

two black snakes grew from the shoulders of the king. As often as he cut them off, they grew again until the devil, this time in the form of a doctor, said that the only remedy was to feed the snakes every day with human brains.

As Zahhak increased in power Jamshid's authority declined and men proclaimed Zahhak the monarch of Persia. Jamshid went into hiding but was at last found in the sea of China where Zahhak had him sawn in two, thus ridding the world of him. Zahhak's rule lasted for a thousand years, a thousand years of oppression, in which virtue declined, sorcery increased and each day two men died that their brains might be fed to the serpents who grew from Zahhak's shoulders.

But all was not well for Zahhak. In a dream he foresaw the birth of Faridun (Thraetaona) and sought to have the child destroyed, but in vain. Fearful of so mighty an opponent, Zahhak commanded that an army of demons be gathered to attack his enemy and a proclamation made to affirm his virtue as king. No one dared oppose so mighty a monarch, until one day a humble blacksmith, wronged by the king, appeared at court seeking a just release for his imprisoned son. He proclaimed

Although you have a dragon's form, you are a king and it is your duty to let me have justice.
Levy, p. 18

The king was astonished at the outburst and acceded to his request but sought in return his signature of the proclamation. The blacksmith, a brave and forthright man, refused, denounced the king, and with his son raised an army for Faridun from the market place. His banner was a strip of leather decorated with jewels and for Faridun he prepared a mace with an ox's head. Leaving his palace whose pinnacles reached the skies, Faridun led his forces through torrents and over deserts to the palace

of the wicked king in Jerusalem. Unafraid at the sight of the palace which reached up to the planet Saturn, he grasped his mace and advanced. Zahhak was absent, but on hearing of Faridun's invasion and the setting free of Jamshid's sisters he rode at breathtaking speed before a mighty army. With his army before the city Zahhak entered the palace himself, unrecognised in his heavy armour. As he approached the women with murder in his heart Faridun 'advanced upon him with the speed of a storm wind' and smashed his helmet with his mace. Warned by an angel, he refrained from killing the evil tyrant, but bound him and with trusted companions carried him off to Mount Demavend. Now ruler of the world, Faridun turned his attention to improving the lot of men. His old mythological assault on disease is transformed, or demythologised, and becomes instead an agricultural act of overcoming pestilence with husbandry.

Here we must leave the narrative of the *Shah name* and the 'history' that it reconstructs from the ancient myths. But the process of interpreting myth as history is one which continues in Zoroastrianism and in the minds of the faithful of many religions to the present day. A famous Parsi scholar, for example, suggests that Haoma, plant and god, was

a great man of Iran, who had done some great deeds that commemorated his name.
Modi, RC., p. 301

Myth and history are, then, completely intertwined in Zoroastrian belief. The Persians understand the whole of their history, past, present and future, in the light of their mythology. History is the stage for the battle between good and evil and the events which take place on that stage can only be truly appreciated when seen against the backcloth of God's purpose and nature.

Opposite These fire altars at Naqsh-i Rustam date from Sasanian times. Although the building of fire temples was by then a long-standing tradition, these altars show how the ancient tradition of worshipping on mountain tops (page 24) was preserved even at major royal sites in the mighty days of empire. Indeed, it is still part of the living tradition in the twentieth century. Bibliothèque Nationale, Paris.

Above Faridun enthroned in a flower garden after his victory over Zahhak. Bibliothèque Nationale, Paris.

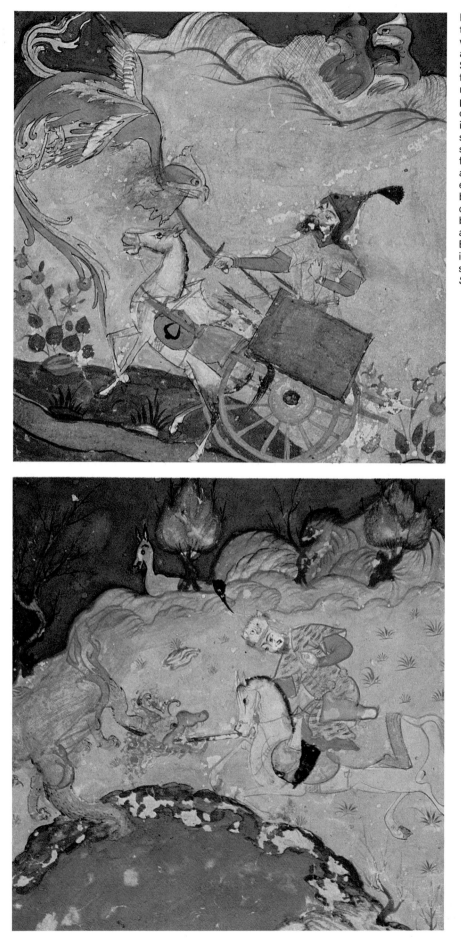

Rustam is a legendary hero of Persian tradition. He was not born in the normal way but as a result of the incantations of a wizard at the behest of the mythological Simurgh bird with the aid of its magical feathers. A lion of a man, as tall as eight men, he rode a horse of magnificent prowess. After searching the country he caught one set aside for him from birth; it had the strength of an elephant and the speed of a racing camel. Famed for his strength, Rustam saved his monarchs from prison. He slew dragons, demons and great warriors in battle, himself enduring treachery, attack, even capture by demons. On one occasion he was dropped into the ocean among monsters but escaped and finally triumphed. The author is indebted to Professor Sir Harold Bailey for permission to reproduce these illustrations from an unpublished seventeenth-century manuscript of the *Shah name* from Bukhara.

Opposite, top The mythological bird Simurgh and the ambitious prince Isfandiyar, who was defeated by Rustam with Simurgh's help.

Opposite bottom Rustam defeating a dragon in order to save his monarch, King Kavus.

Right, above Rustam, led by the captive Awlad to the demons' abode, overpowers the Great White Demon in order to save King Kavus.

Right, below To capture Rustam the demon Akwan took away the ground on which the hero slept and then threw him into the ocean.

Myth, Ritual and Symbolism

Myth and ritual are intertwined in all religions, nowhere more so than in Zoroastrianism. Many of the texts, certainly all the ancient ones, have been preserved precisely because they are used in the ritual. Equally the rituals commonly have their explanation in the myths. An account of a mythology which did not include a chapter on the interconnectedness between myth and ritual would be leaving a very serious gap. Similarly much of the symbolism in a religion is stimulated by the mythology, and the reverse is also true.

Zoroastrian rites are rarely explained in detail in the ancient texts, but it is evident that the living practices are both grounded in and very faithful to extremely ancient traditions, so that it is perfectly reasonable to interpret the one in the light of the other. In this chapter much of the account is based on the Zoroastrian practices of the Indian Parsis, because of the author's work with that community.

The Zoroastrian understanding of the purpose of prayer and ritual is different from that readily familiar in the West, especially from the Protestant tradition. In the latter prayer is often understood as a form of dialogue with God; this can be part of Zoroastrian worship and seems to have been part of the prophet's own practice, but it is not the primary understanding of prayer in Zoroastrianism. Prayers are recited in the holy language of *Avesta* both because it is the language of Zoroaster and revelation and because Zoroastrians believe they are words of spiritual power. The holy words when 'put into practice', that is said by a holy man, are considered effective and alive, whereas when they are printed in books, or left unsaid, they are dead. The priest must recite the holy words with utter devotion and attentiveness. These words then make the forces they refer to present and active. It is not simply that the words point to realities beyond the descriptive power of human language. It is more that they bring about the real presence of those powers. The properly recited prayers to the Bounteous Immortals effect the presence of those beings. The myth becomes alive and effective here and now. The heavenly beings come to dwell in the place of the enacted rite.

Ritual acts are effective sources of power that aid the gods as well as men. So, as we have seen (pp. 25–6), Tishtrya is unable to defeat the demon of drought and produce the life-giving waters until a sacrifice has been offered to him. Similarly Zurvan, when wanting a son, offered sacrifice although he himself is the absolute and there is no one to whom he could present his offerings. A sacrifice offered with devotion is one of the most meritorious acts a Zoroastrian can perform. Without sacrifice the world would cease to exist, but by it the power of Ahriman is reduced. At the renovation men will be made immortal through a sacrifice offered by Ohrmazd himself. This understanding of sacrifice, still dominant in Zoroastrianism, dates back to Indo-Iranian times, for sacrifice is central to the religion of the earliest of Indian texts, the *Vedas*, where duly performed rituals are thought to be effective independent of the will of the gods. In Zoroastrian ritual every word and action is imbued with the highest significance.

It is impossible in a short book to consider the inter-connection between myth and all the rituals of Zoroastrianism. Instead we shall look at three of the most important of the rituals practised by the layperson, those concerned with initiation, fire and death.

Traditionally, initiation takes place at the age of puberty, though nowadays children undergo *Naujote* (understood to mean 'new birth') a little younger. Infants are not thought to be morally responsible for their thoughts, words and deeds because they cannot tell the difference between right and wrong. Initiation takes place when the child can so distinguish. Hereafter the child is responsible for its actions which will be stored and weighed on the day of judgment. Initiation is, therefore, into the responsibilities of the religion. It is also considered to be voluntary enrollment into the army of God.

Basically the ceremony consists of a preliminary purificatory bath to cleanse the body with prayers and the drinking of cow's urine (*gomez*) for inner cleanliness. The ceremony proper is conducted by a senior priest with assistants. It commences with a declaration of faith and then the first ritual putting on of the sacred shirt (*sudre*) and cord (*kusti*). These are commonly referred to as the armour of God and should be worn by the initiate throughout his or her life. The child recites for the first time the prayers that he or she (there is no difference between the sexes in ritual duties) will say several times daily until death. The *Naujote* ends with the priest blessing the child.

The *sudre* is a white cotton garment, rather like a vest. It is white

as a symbol of the purity of the religion. At the front 'V' of the neck there is a small symbolic or spiritual purse, the *Kissa eh Kerfeh* in which the initiate should store up good thoughts, words and deeds. At the centre back of the neck there is a doubling of the cloth, the *girdo*, to remind the Zoroastrian to carry his or her own load of duties and responsibilities.

The *kusti* is a long cord woven, traditionally, by a priest's wife, from lamb's wool, though camel and goat wool were used in times past. It is spoken of in ancient texts as 'the star-studded girdle of the spirit fashioned good religion'. It consists of seventy-two threads which are said to

The late High priest of the Zoroastrian Association of Europe, Dastur Dr. Kutar tending the fire in the boi ceremony in the London prayer room. The author wishes to express his gratitude to the Association for permission to photograph the community at worship and for their consistent help with his research. The sanctuary is designed on traditional Parsi lines. It is marked off by floor to ceiling walls with bar windows through which the worshippers see and reverence the fire – some of them can be seen on the far side of the sanctuary. The fire is spoken of as the Son of God, the representative of God on earth, a living, divinely created, formless icon of the source of all light and life-giving warmth.

Three famous Parsi temples. *Above* The Atash Bahram in Navsari. The fire was consecrated in 1765, but the present building dates only from 1925. This temple is the seat of the senior of all Parsi priests, Dastur Meherji Rana. Architectural details are again based on motifs from Persepolis and Naqsh-i Rustam. *Opposite, top* The Goti fire temple is just outside Surat. This is quite a centre of pilgrimage as miracles are thought to happen there. The third temple (*opposite, bottom*) is at Udwada a small, peaceful, coastal village which has become perhaps *the* centre of Parsi pilgrimage, because it houses the fire consecrated by the original settlers from Persia in the tenth century and has burned continuously ever since. The present building was erected in 1894 as an act of charity by the Wadia family.

Hinduism also as the badge of the priest. It has been plausibly argued that it was the prophet Zoroaster himself who 'democratized' the *kusti*, and so made it the badge of all believers.

A selection from the *kusti* prayers, first recited at *Naujote*, illustrates the preservation of ancient concepts and myths in the living tradition. The child is unlikely to be able to translate the *Avestan* prayers, but most initiates have a general understanding of their meaning and importance. The following includes the opening of the covered (*Fravarane*) and the *Ohrmazd Khoday*, two of the kusti prayers.

I profess myself a Mazda-worshipper and follower of Zarathushtra, I pledge myself to the well thought thought . . . to the well spoken word . . . to the well acted act. . . .
Ohrmazd is Lord! Ahriman he keeps at bay. . . .
May Ahriman be struck and defeated, with devs and drujs, sorcerers and sinners . . . tyrants, wrongdoers and heretics, sinners, enemies and witches! May they all be struck and defeated. . . .
O Ohrmazd, Lord! I am contrite for all sins and I desist from them all, from all bad thoughts, bad words and bad acts which I have thought, spoken or done in the world, or which have happened through me, or have originated with me. For those sins . . .
I am contrite, I renounce them. . . .
With satisfaction for Ahura Mazda, scorn for Angra Mainyu! . . . I praise Asha [Righteousness].
Boyce, Sources, pp. 58f.

represent the seventy-two chapters of the sacred text and ritual the *yasna* (pp. 33–34), and the seventy-two names of God given in the ancient hymn (*Yasht*) to Him. It has three tassels at each end, the total of six represents the six great festivals (*gahambars*). The woven 'tube' of the *kusti* when pressed flat has an upper and lower layer representing sky and earth with the central hollow symbolic of the atmosphere in between. The *kusti* is tied round the waist three times symbolising good thoughts, words and deeds. In later learned priestly tradition the strands, tassels and threads became invested with very involved symbolism. But the cord and its essential meaning almost certainly go back to Indo-Iranian tradition, as it appears in

Thus underlying the rite of initiation is the traditional myth and understanding of the dualistic battle, the traditions associated with pollution and purification, the theme of judgment of the individual and the belief in individual free will. Myth and ritual are interwoven; it is largely through the ritual that the initiate learns of the myth. So closely related are they that the one cannot be understood by the outsider without the other.

Ritual Fire

The Zoroastrian myth concerning the personification of Fire, Atar, has already been discussed (pp. 30–31). We can now look at the mythology of some of the sacred fires of the ritual. Most religions try to trace the origins of their great centres of ritual back to the early times of their sacred history. The Zoroastrians try to trace their three most famous fires back to primeval history. These three fires are the Farnbag fire, which is said to have been situated either in Kabul in modern Afghanistan or Kanya in Persia; the Gushnasp fire, which was probably situated in Shiz; and the Burzen Mihr fire, which was situated on Mount Revand in the north west of Nishapur. All three are said to have been carried on the back of the mythical ox, Srishok, in the reign of the primeval Takhmoruw. One night there was a great storm and the fires were blown off the ox's back into the sea where they continued to burn and give light to men at sea. Each fire is associated with one of the three classes of society: the Farnbag with the priests, the Gushnasp with the warriors and the Burzen Mihr with the productive workers. All three helped Yima in his paradisal kingdom and it was Yima who installed the Farnbag fire in its due place. When his glory fell it was that fire which saved his glory from the evil Dahak. The Burzen Mihr fire protected the world until the time of Zoroaster's patron, Vishtaspa, preparing the way for the great revelation and itself performing miracles during the great monarch's rule. The Gushnasp fire is said to have preserved the world until the time of the great Sasanian king, Khusrau. When he destroyed idol temples the fire settled on his horse's mane dispelling the darkness and gloom. These three great fires, then, are not thought to have been simply late historical innovations but are rather the protectors and guides for men throughout history.

There are three classes of ritual fires: Bahram fires, the Adaran fires and the Dadgah fires. The Bahram is the victorious king of fires. It is invoked, in the name of Ohrmazd, to give strength against the forces of darkness for its glory does battle with the Lie, standing as it does as a symbol of righteousness. The fire is enthroned rather than installed and the wood is set out in the pattern of a throne. Over it hangs a crown expressing the sovereignty of the mighty fire. When it has been enthroned it is carried in triumph like a king by four priests in procession, while others hold a canopy over it. Before and behind proceed priests with swords and maces of Mithra, all forming a royal bodyguard. Once enthroned it can only be tended by priests who have undergone the most rigorous purification rites. No one but they can enter the sanctuary and even they must tend it with white-gloved hands. The reason for its sanctity is the great process of purification. Sixteen fires are gathered from different sources and then purified a total of 1,128 times, a process which takes about a year. The cost involved is enormous and not surprisingly such a fire is very rarely enthroned. There are two Atash Bahrams in Iran and eight in India. Buildings housing such fires are sometimes referred to as 'cathedral Fire Temples'.

Ordinary fire temples, properly *Dar-i Mihrs*, in India are often called *Agiaris* (Gujarati for house of fire). In them burn fires of the second and third grades. The Adaran and Dadgah fires are much less grand affairs. The latter can even be tended by a layman when kept at home. Both are installed with martial honours for the sacred fires represent the spiritual rule of light and truth in the war against the powers of darkness, a battle which the faithful must fight in conjunction with Ohrmazd and his son, Fire.

The ritual fire in the temple represents to Zoroastrians the special place where God's presence is experienced. The divine is present in all forms of fire, in all correctly performed rites and in all his good creations. But, as with most religions, he is to be particularly found in the temple sanctuary. There, in purity, the worshipper stands in the presence of God.

Before entering the temple proper,

Opposite The Anjuman Atash Bahram, Bombay. This is the most recent of the great 'cathedral' fire temples to be built. It was built from community (Anjuman) subscription and was consecrated in 1898. The high priesthood of this temple is in the line of the JamaspAsas, one of the three senior priestly families of the traditional priestly city of Navsari. Non-Parsis cannot enter the ritual centres of any temple which, because of the lay out of the building in this case, means the gateway. The architectural style is a mixture of Victorian interpretation of Greek architecture and some traditional Persian motifs, for example bull-headed columns over the portico (*see* page 93); the winged figure and the fires atop the balustrade from those of Naqsh-i Rustam (see page 14). In this building the ground floor is used for prayer and other ritual rooms and the upstairs for more public occasions such as lectures, weddings and initiations.

This sequence shows the naujotes of Rushna and Anahita Avari in Manchester in 1984.

Above The priests lead Rushna and Anahita from their home to the hall where the initiation is to be performed. At home they had cleansed themselves physically and spiritually by washing and prayer, and put on traditional white clothing as a token of purity. Senior lady family members follow carrying a tray on which there are various items for the ceremony, such as their *sudre* and *kusti*, the sacred shirt and cord. In the hall (*above, right*) Rushna and Anahita sit facing the officiating priests who lit the fire which is present at all Zoroastrian ceremonies representing the divine presence. On the tray is a small oil lamp, tokens of good fortune and pieces of sandalwood with which the fire is fed. The two naujotes are performed simultaneously. *Right* The priests invest the sisters with their *sudres*.

Left Then Rushna recites her prayers guided by the priest. After that (*below left*) the *kusti* is tied on officially for the first time. *Below right* Thus invested with the armour and sword belt of their religion these two new recruits in the army of Ahura Mazda sit before the priests who shower them with rice (symbolic of good life) and bless them. There are no grades of initiation (other than for the priesthood) in Zoroastrianism, so Rushna and Anahita are now full members of the religion, with the duties and joys that membership entails. The naujote is the same for girls as for boys.

Zoroastrians purify themselves physically by washing and spiritually by prayer. In the outer rooms of the temple are pictures of the heroes of the faith to inspire the worshipper. Women enter temples the same as men, except during their periods of menstruation (p. 56). Both men and women have their heads covered as a token of respect and do not wear their shoes lest they carry in any impurity from the outside world. In the prayer room the fire is kept ever burning by being fed five times each day. It burns in a censer, inside a sanctuary marked off by floor-to-ceiling walls with doors and a window so that the faithful can pay their respects, meditate upon and pray before the fire. Only a ritually pure priest may enter the sanctuary. Normally a worshipper offers a gift of wood to the fire, by leaving it on a tray for the priest to offer on his behalf, and takes and applies to his forehead a pinch of ash left in a holder in the doorway. Stepping back, the worshipper prays silently and individually. There is no real concept of congregational worship in Zoroastrianism. As every person has individual responsibility for their actions and destiny so also man approaches God individually.

But prayer is not offered only, or even most frequently, in a temple. The *kusti* prayers can be said anywhere. They are said facing a light, the symbol of God, and before one of God's other creations, notably the waters. There is a deep conviction in Zoroastrianism that man should worship before God's creations, not man's. Temple worship was a fairly late entry to Zoroastrianism, not

beginning until approximately the fourth century B.C. and in many ways it has always remained optional. But in practice temple attendance is popular, for there, in purity, man stands alone before the son of God, the representative of Ohrmazd, a living formless icon.

The Funerary Rites

The funerary rites of Zoroastrianism are very clearly governed by the mythology. Death, it will be remembered, is the work of the devil in Zoroastrian belief. It is his triumph over the Good Creation. A dead body is, therefore, the abode of demons. The more righteous the deceased the greater the triumph of Ahriman and the greater the demonic power necessary to achieve it. Hence the corpse of a holy man is a far greater source of defilement than that of a wicked man whose death was easily achieved. Many of the funerary rites are concerned with purification from the contamination which is the work of demons. Since a corpse is such a source of defilement, it cannot be allowed to be buried for fear of contaminating the sacred element of the earth, nor can it be burned for fear of defiling the fire. Where this is not possible, for example because there are no vultures, the preferred method of disposal is to use a stone coffin so that the pollution does not affect the earth. Nowadays Zoroastrians living in America or Britain often choose cremation, arguing that in modern crematoria it is not a flame but intense heat generated by electricity which consumes the body.

If it is known that a person is dying

a priest should be called to recite the confession and a fire brought into the room so that the forces of darkness associated with death may be kept at bay. At death the body should be washed with *gomez*, considered the most powerful earthly cleansing agent, and dressed in a clean *sudre* and *kusti* (waste is a Zoroastrian sin). As it is believed that the demon of putrefaction and decay, Nasu, takes possession of the body the priest and family keep at a distance; only professional corpse-bearers (*nasarsalas*) handle it. Because of their contact with death they are considered unclean and do not mix freely in society. On retirement they may undergo a nine-day purification ceremony (*bareshnom*) after which they can again mix easily. The corpse-bearers mark a space around the body with nails into which circle others must not enter for fear of pollution. A dog is brought in to perform the *sagdid*; it views the body to verify death or guard against the evil forces thought to be powerfully present. Prayers then commence until the time of the funeral. If possible this occurs on the day of death, but as funerals may not take place after sunset – the time of darkness when traditionally evil powers prowl and may attack the living – it sometimes has to be delayed until the following day. If, necessary, prayers must be said through the night with a priest and family member in the room with the corpse. One should not stand alone and unprotected when evil is such a strong presence. At set intervals during the night the dog is brought in to perform further *sagdids*.

At the appointed time the funeral procession forms with everyone in pairs and holding a white cloth (*paiwand*) between them to bind them together for strength to resist evil. As the body is lifted on to the bier priests and mourners turn away, closing nose and mouth lest the infection of evil spreads at the movement. The corpse's face is left uncovered; the rest of the body is covered in a shroud. The bier is made of metal; porous substances such as wood are never brought into contact with a dead body lest they soak up the pollution. The corpse-bearers are followed by two priests and then the mourners in pairs. They proceed in silence. Normally only men go to the Tower of silence, the *daxma*. Near the *daxma* the corpse is laid on a marble slab (again non-porous) for the mourners to take their leave of the deceased by having a last glimpse of the face. A *sagdid* is performed, then the corpse-bearers, and they alone, take the body up the steps into the *daxma* and expose it to the vultures. The mourners watch the procession to the *daxma* then return to a nearby building while they say certain prayers. These last for less than half an hour, during which time the corpse will normally have been devoured. On returning home mourners wash and pray to cleanse them from the impurity so virulently present at death and then return to their daily life. The family offer appropriate ceremonies at specified intervals over the following year, but particularly for the first three days.

The belief in the passage of the soul in the first three days after death

determines the rites which are performed. As it is Sraosha who protects the soul during this time, prayers are offered to him during the five divisions of the day by two or more priests and the relatives both at home and in the Fire-Temple. The most important of these prayers is the one offered on the third day when the soul passes to its judgment. Then the blessing of the Almighty is sought and ceremonies are offered to the angels concerned with the judgment.

Many Westerners view the rite of exposing the dead to vultures with horror. Zoroastrians view Western graveyards with equal horror, pointing out how much longer the same process takes. *Daxmas*, they maintain, are more natural, more hygienic and less wasteful of space.

The rites for the deceased do not end three days after death, but the stress is not on continued mourning. Excessive mourning is a sin in Zoroastrianism for it is of no help to the soul, it can harm the body of the living, and is pointless in view of the belief in a life after death and the assurance of the resurrection. Zoroastrians have a strong sense of communion with the dead, who are invited to share in the feastings of the living, not in grief but in companiable happiness, 'for the rejoicing of the soul'. A scholar who has lived among the Zoroastrians gives an interesting insight into this attitude:

After I had enjoyed for some time the hospitality of Irani Zoroastrians, but before I had begun to comprehend this feeling for the dead, I ventured, still haunted by

A visit to a temple for a Parsi to worship is basically a pilgrimage. These illustrations follow that pilgrimage route at the D. N. Modi Atash Bahram in Surat. The author wishes to express his profound gratitude to the temple's authorities for permitting him to enter (when the fire had been removed for building renovations), the first time (as far as known) for such access to be granted a Western scholar. The entrance hall (*opposite left*) is decorated with pictures of distinguished Zoroastrians and of the prophet himself, to inspire the worshipper. Through a succession of doors (*opposite middle*) the faithful pass on to the prayer room (*opposite right*) which is striking in its simplicity. In this temple the prayer room is walled with Italian marble and the only decoration is the motif of the bull capital from Persepolis on the columns (*opposite right* and *above left*). Inside, the sanctuary is tiled white to ensure the cleanliness that is an important part of holiness in Zoroastrianism. Dirt is associated with decay and is, therefore, part of the process of death and impurity which is evil's weapon. The *afringan* or altar in which the fire normally burns is as high as a man. In the background can be seen the bell which is struck during the *boi* ceremony of feeding the fire five times daily (*above middle*). In an Atash Bahram, a 'cathedral' fire temple, the fire is considered of such sanctity that no artificial light should dim its glory, so that in the day only sunlight enters the sanctuary and in the night it burns alone, a powerful expression of the holy. The Zoroastrian prays standing in dignity, but with head covered and shoes off as token of respect before the fire (*above right*).

associations of death with sorrow,
to ask if they never celebrated a feast
day without an accompanying ritual
for the dead. The reply, made with
mild astonishment, was: 'But of
course not. We always want them to
share in our happiness.'
M.B. Pious Foundations, p. 247, n4

The Zoroastrian mythology of the individual and universal judgments, as we have seen, thus dictates both the funerary rites and their attitude to festivities.

The Understanding of Myth and Ritual

The ancient myths of Zoroastrianism, as in almost all religions, remain the mainspring of the daily religious life of the faithful. They provide the justification for actions, however the modern intellectual may re-interpret or adapt the tradition. Naturally the leaders claim that their symbolic interpretation of the myth is both relevant to man's daily life and true to the original intention of the myth. In what religion would one dare to suggest that the interpretation given to a particular myth was not that of the founder but a completely new idea!

In the preservation of the ancient practices Zoroastrianism provides a particularly good example of the conservative character of ritual. What we have seen in Zoroastrianism is only a form writ large of what may be observed in most religions, including those of the West. Zoroastrianism is, as we shall see, very much a common-sense religion in its understanding of man and the world; it is profound and rather philosophical. That it can also retain such a traditional and conservative attitude to its myth and ritual makes it an interesting 'case book' to study. It contains a number of particularly clear examples of how religions tend to develop. The modern critical mind finds it difficult, if not impossible, to accept some of the myths and rituals of the traditional faiths, yet equally the faithful will not reject them. Instead they resort to allegory or symbolism, be it symbolic

interpretation of the Book of *Genesis* or of the *Avesta*. The attempts of a modern Parsi to interpret the *Avesta* in modern terms rather than reject it is an interesting phenomenon which could be paralleled in many religions. Such a Parsi writes:

Some portions of the Avesta, *if taken literally, would seem absurd. Mountains, rivers and similar topographical features do not refer to any physical locations, but probably to some psycho-physiological features, some psychic currents within the human body (brain, nerves or some plexus or gland, etc.).*
Quoted D-G, *Symbols*, p. 19

There is a lot of truth in the saying that as critical reflection develops symbolism tends to expand (Duchesne-Guillemin). This is true of the quotation just given and true of the Zoroastrian ritual, although we should not forget that the ancient mind also made extensive use of symbolism. Not all symbolic interpretations are necessarily modern.

In Zoroastrianism, then, myth and ritual are completely intertwined. The one supports, explains and justifies the other. Both preserve extremely ancient views of the world and of man's part in it. Yet neither are merely expressions of opinion. They are, together, effective sources of power which, if properly recited and performed by men, themselves endowed with due power, bring benefit and merit to the individual in life, protection at death and the promise of future bliss, and uphold the very existence of the universe. The vital nature of ritual action demands that everything be performed in precisely the right way. A wrong action,

Opposite Zoroastrians offer prayer not only before fire but also before water; both are divine creations. The sinking of this well in central Bombay was, therefore, a particular act of charity for it provided a place both of spiritual and physical succour in a busy, hot city. The seats in welcome shade provide a place of rest. Around the well Parsis, heads covered as a token of worshipful respect, offer prayer. In a side room oil lamps, small fires, may be lit and left burning as indicators of the faithful person's wish to continue in prayer. Those who have the time may also offer their prayers (*above*) before the picture of the prophet.

a mistake at any stage, could vitiate the whole act. The rituals are of such a sacred and potent character that unbelieving eyes cannot be allowed to see them.

Within the Zoroastrian ritual one can see the basic Zoroastrian beliefs, which are expressed in narrative form in the myths, acted out by the believers in the ritual. Zoroastrianism is a religion concerned with war, war against the powers of evil. The history of the world is, mythically speaking, a battle between good and evil: between God and the devil. So in the installation of the sacred fires, the symbol of the presence of God, martial imagery is very much to the fore as it is in the rite of initiation. It is also a religion of hope. This hope is expressed in narrative form in the myths of the triumph of good over evil at the renovation, and is implicit in the ritual with its greater emphasis on prayers and rituals intended to aid the soul, than on mourning, and its joyous invitation to the deceased to share in feasts.

To the modern Western mind the Zoroastrian attitude towards the ritual may appear rather magical. To the Zoroastrian the acts they perform have such power because they follow the pattern of a heavenly model, because they effectively unite the divine and human worlds, a common theme in their mythology. In view of

their belief in the power of the ritual it is understandable that they should be reluctant to change its form, although in the interpretation given to their actions and myths we can see the modern critical mind at work.

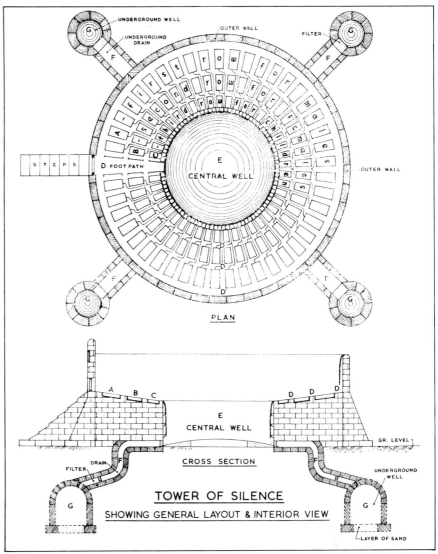

TOWER OF SILENCE
SHOWING GENERAL LAYOUT & INTERIOR VIEW

Opposite, top left Before entering a fire temple the worshipper purchases a piece of sweet-smelling sandalwood to offer to the fire. The entrances are commonly garlanded with flowers and the floor decorated with auspicious symbols used on festive occasions in India. A place of worship is, in Zoroastrian belief, a place of happiness and is decorated accordingly. Near the entrance a place is set aside for washing the exposed portions of the body (*opposite, top right*). So the worshipper enters the temple in a state of physical purity prior to the spiritual cleansing through prayer. (*opposite left middle*). The *kusti* is untied and held out in prayer as the believer rejects Ahriman and all his works, affirms belief in Ohrmazd and vows to practice good thoughts, words and deeds. The *kusti* is then retied.

Above, left A *bareshnum gah* where the nine-day purification ceremony is performed which cleanses a person of real impurity. It is necessary for a priest before he can serve in a temple sanctuary and has to be renewed if he vitiates that purity. The nine days are spent in prayer, meditation and washings upon these stones where the impurity will be kept from the good earth. The author wishes to express his gratitude to the authorities in Surat for granting permission for his visit (normally forbidden) and permission to photograph.

Above Inside this, (and many), *daxmas* there are three concentric circles of places (*pavis*) marked out in which the bodies are laid – men, women and children on the inner circle. Drain channels take away liquids to a central pit where the bones are also cast after they have been bleached and powdered by the sun. Acid is poured into the pit to ensure all is destroyed. Underground channels carry away all waste.

A *daxma* (*opposite, bottom*) from the priestly city of Navsari.

Conclusion: Myth and Belief

The Understanding of God, the World and Man

Myth, we have said, is important for what it means to the believer, for the reflections it contains on man's views on himself, the world and God. Myths are not bogus historical narratives. One must leave behind the outer shell of myth and look at the kernel. What is the kernel of Persian mythology and what views on life do the myths contain?

To a Zoroastrian, God is wholly good. Being fundamentally opposed to evil He can have no contact with it and is, throughout history, engaged in a life and death struggle with it. God is the source of all that is good, the creator of the heavens, the world and man, the source of life, health, beauty and joy. Evil is a reality, but a wholly negative force seeking to destroy, corrupt and defile. Death, disease, misery and sin are all the work of the devil who seeks to annihilate God's world.

The world is created by God as an aid in the battle against evil. He is a rational being and has a reason for all that he does. He does not create the world merely for sport, as in some branches of Hinduism, nor does he repent of it as the God of the Hebrew scriptures so often does. The world may be the battleground between good and evil, but it is essentially good, and when not corrupted by evil it displays the characteristics of its creator — orderliness and harmony. To deny the essential goodness of the material world is one of the gravest sins a Zoroastrian can commit. Doctrines which teach that the flesh is evil, that the body is a prison of the soul or of original sin are verbiage to a Zoroastrian. Therefore, he does not look to the final subjugation of the body or of matter, but to the ideal union of matter and spirit; he looks not for the end of the world, but for the renovation of God's world.

The creation and eschatological myths of Zoroastrianism provide the ultimate charter for the daily lives of the faithful. If the world belongs to God then it would be a sin for them to withdraw from it by becoming monks or ascetics. If God is characterised by creativity and increase then men have a religious duty to work for the increase of the Good Creation through agriculture, industry and marriage. Celibacy is a sin for it fails to expand the Good Creation. Abortion and homosexuality are sins, for they prevent the true purpose of the sexual act, the increase of the Good Creation, just as effectively as the sinful abstinence of man's first parents did. Disease and ill-health are blights with which the devil afflicted the world at the beginning. Men, therefore, have a religious duty to preserve their bodies in a state of health. Man is composed of five elements — soul, vital spirit (the principle of life), *fravashi* (his heavenly self), consciousness and body, but he is a unity. Spiritual and physical health, therefore, go hand in hand. The idea that spiritual progress can be made by suppressing the body through fasting is sheer folly to the

A bull-headed mace of Mithra carried by Zoroastrian priests as a symbol of the war they must wage against the forces of evil. Mithra shakes his mace over hell three times each day to restrain the demons from inflicting greater punishment on the damned than they merit.

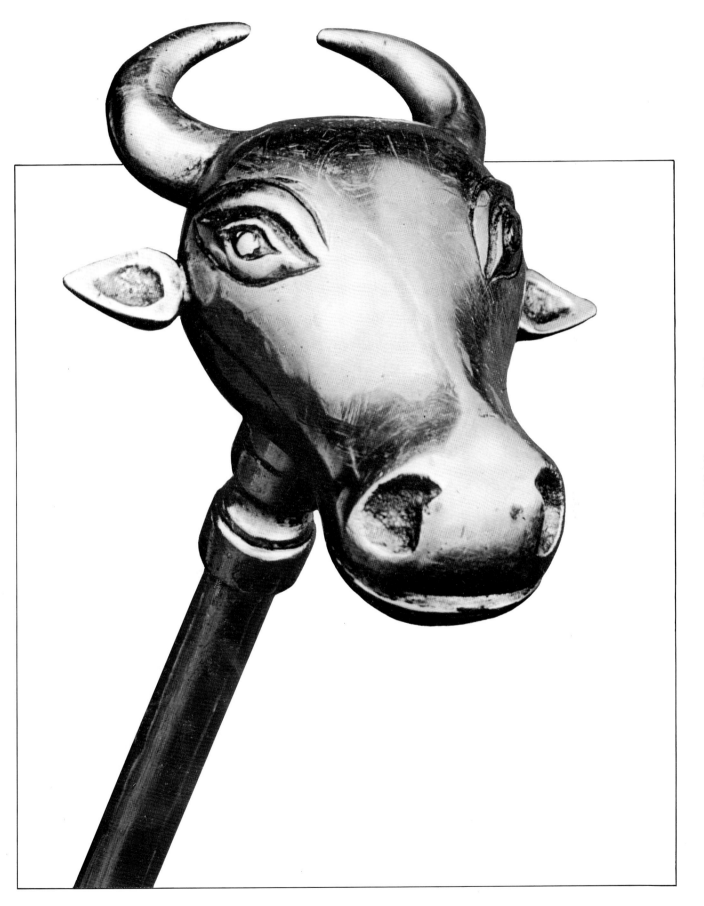

Zoroastrian. Since the material world belongs to God, material success that is gained honestly, without hurt to others, and is coupled with generosity, is an aid, not a hindrance, to spiritual progress. Unlike many of the contemplative schools of Hinduism, Zoroastrianism has an activist ethic. Idleness is of the devil and

work is the salt of life. Without work our life is idle and useless. Our religion teaches us that work is the aim and object of life. We must always keep our body ready and healthy for doing the duties of our life, to do good and right deeds, to help others and to fight against ignorance, evil and misery in the world.
Modi Catechism, p. 30

It was the devil who afflicted the world with misery. The religious attitude to life is, therefore, one of joy. On the day of the month that is dedicated to God the faithful are exhorted to 'drink wine and be merry', and on the day dedicated to Rashnu, the god of judgment, 'life is gay: do in holiness anything you will.' (*Counsels of Adherbadh ZT.* pp. 107f.)

Debauchery, drunkenness and licence are, of course, equally condemned for all must be governed by the Golden Mean, by the motto 'all things in moderation'.

Man, as the great creation and ally of God, is the particular object for the onslaughts of evil. It is the duty of the faithful to overcome these assaults, to

overcome doubts and unrighteous desires with reason, overcome greed with contentment, anger with serenity, envy with benevolence, want with vigilance, strife with peace, falsehood with truth.
Counsels of the Sages, ZT p. 25

The demons may assail man with disease, with all manner of afflictions, even with death, but, like the sinless Gayomart before him, man must always hold fast to the religion. This means more than just a faithful observance of the ritual and the reading of the sacred scriptures. Because the material world, the body and happiness are the creation of God, it is man's religious duty to preserve, expand and enjoy them all.

This is the path of Truth. He who follows it is a follower of Truth, an

asha-van, a member of the Good Religion. But Zoroastrians do not believe that men are compelled to do this. The *fravashis* of men are said in the myths to have agreed collectively to fight for Ohrmazd. Freedom of will for the individual is an essential part of Zoroastrianism. The ally of God man may be, but all men have to choose between the Truth and Lie. Once made, the choice has to be re-affirmed continually, for evil ever lurks at hand to mislead and destroy. A doctrine of pre-destination such as flourished in Zurvanism and Islam is held morally repugnant, for it detracts from the justice and goodness of God. Equally repugnant is the idea that one man can die to save all. If everyone is free to adopt good or evil then everyone must be judged according to their own thoughts, words and deeds and not those of another.

Thus the Zoroastrian myths of creation and renovation are not merely narratives concerned with the remote past or distant future. They express the basic view of the God-Man relationship and provide the *rationale* for the conduct of the

faithful. They are accounts of a cosmic battle which each man encounters in his own daily life, in his marriage, in his work and in his religious life.

How, one may ask, does the believer interpret the myths concerning the gods and demons? What understanding of the God-Man relationship do these express? It must be remembered that the names of the divine and demonic powers often reflect abstract ideas, Vohu Manh (Good Mind), and Aka Manah (Evil Mind), Sraosha (Obedience) and Az (Wrong Mindedness). The cosmic battle becomes, then, a battle which each man must wage within himself in order to eject the Destructive Spirit from God's world. If men would expel the demons such as Wrath and Greed from their bodies then Ahriman would not be able to find a place in the world.

It is possible to put Ahriman out of this world in such a way that every person, for his own part, should chase him out of his body, for Ahriman's habitation in the world is in the bodies of men. Therefore when there is no habitation for him in the bodies of men, he is annihilated from the whole world. For as long as in this world (even) a small demon has his dwelling in a single person of men, Ahriman is in the world.

Dk. M. 6, 264, Shaked, Notes, p. 230

The duty of the Zoroastrian is not only stated in negative terms of expelling demons from one's self, it is also stated positively. The gods must be made to live in the bodies of men. The abstract qualities which represent the divine powers, Good Mind, Obedience, Truth, must be realised in the daily lives of men if men are to obtain the highest goal, if they are to be united with the gods. In one text it is said that the god whom the individual worships and reverences becomes the soul of that worshipper. When a man is activated by a particular spirit, be that spirit good or evil, then he becomes the material dwelling-place of that spirit and the worldly manifestation of its nature. Thus the battle between the gods and demons is seen as a battle between the passions and tensions at work in the individual. Man's innermost fears and problems are interpreted in the light of the cosmic process. This interpretation of myth, almost taking the myth out of mythology, 'de-mythologising' as modern theologians call it, may not have been the popular or general interpretation of the myths, as the demythologising of the New Testament is not the interpretation of the mass of people in most Christian churches. It may, however, be a very old tradition and appears to be the faith of Zoroaster himself. When Zoroaster speaks of the Bounteous Immortals, the archangels of later Zoroastrianism, the mythological

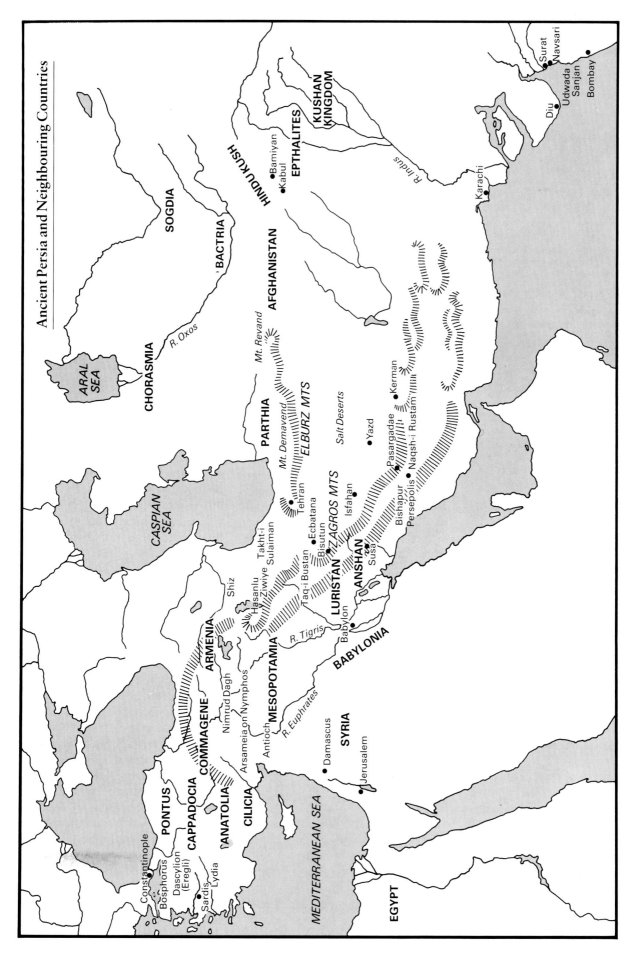

Ancient Persia and Neighbouring Countries

KUSHAN KINGDOM

EPTHALITES

HINDUKUSH

SOGDIA

BACTRIA

AFGHANISTAN

• Bamiyan
• Kabul

R. Indus

Surat
Navsari
Diu
Udwada
Sanjan
Bombay

Karachi

CHORASMIA

R. Oxos

ARAL
SEA

Mt. Revand

PARTHIA

Mt. Demavend

ELBURZ MTS

Salt Deserts

Kerman

Yazd

Pasargadae

Naqsh-i Rustam

CASPIAN
SEA

Tehran

Ecbatana

ZAGROS MTS

Bisutun

Isfahan

Bishapur

Persepolis

Takht-i
Sulaiman

Shiz

Hasanlu

Ziwiye

Taq-i Bustan

LURISTAN

ANSHAN

Susa

ARMENIA

Nimrud Dagh

MESOPOTAMIA

R. Tigris

Babylon

BABYLONIA

COMMAGENE

Arsameia on Nymphos

Antioch

R. Euphrates

SYRIA

• Damascus

• Jerusalem

PONTUS

CAPPADOCIA

CILICIA

ANATOLIA

Constantinople
Bosphorus
Dascylion
(Eregli)

Sardis

Lydia

MEDITERRANEAN SEA

EGYPT

element is negligible. He declares that whoever obeys Ahura Mazda

shall attain wholeness (Haurvatat) and immortality (Ameretat). Mazda is Lord through acts of the Good Spirit.
Ys. 45:5, Boyce, Sources, p. 36

In another place he speaks of the rewards for good deeds and praises

Truth (Asha), Immortality (Ameretat) and the Dominion (Kshathra) of Wholeness (Haurvatat).
Ys. 34:1

Here Zoroaster is speaking of the Entities, God's 'sons and daughters', in a way which is hardly mythological. It is an interpretation of myth which is meaningful to his hearers.

Zoroaster speaks of the Saviours, also, in a non-mythological way. He speaks of them as benefactors (the literal translation of Soshyants).

They truly shall be 'saoshyants' of the lands, who follow knowledge of Thy teaching Mazda, with good purpose, with acts inspired by truth. They indeed have been appointed opponents of Fury.
Ys. 48:12, Boyce, Sources, p. 39

In other words Zoroaster interprets the saviour not simply as a mythological figure but as anyone who works for Wisdom, Truth and the Good Religion in the world, thereby suppressing the disruptive forces at work within man.

Thus both Zoroaster and his followers see in the traditional mythology the pattern of the struggle which every man encounters within himself and in his daily life. Myth is viewed not simply as a narrative of what has happened or will happen; it is not an account of a remote external event, but an interpretation of the problems of human life. Perhaps many Zoroastrians throughout history have taken the myths at their face value, but if we were to look at them only on this simple level we would be doing a great disservice to the profundity which lies at the heart of much Persian mythology.

From ancient times fire has been a central feature of Persian mythology and ritual. It continues to be a focus of Zoroastrian worship to this day. In the times when Zoroastrianism was an imperial religion it was depicted on the tombs of monarchs and on their coins; it was the recipient of lavish gifts in magnificent temples and a centre for worship on the mountains. At ordinary acts of worship and daily devotions, at the higher ceremonies in a temple, weddings, initiations or at funerals, fire is considered the son or representative of God; to be approached in purity and with reverence. Fire is the seventh creation of Ahura Mazda; the one which permeates all others as the expression of light and life. All fire is sacred whether it is the household fire or the sun in the heavens. As a fire of the highest grade (Atash Bahram) is consecrated from sixteen different types of fire (for example, that of a king, of a householder and one ignited by lightning) and all are united in one, so God draws to himself men from all strata of society. As the flames reach upward, so man must reach up to God. Some believe that as man has the spark of the divine fire within him he is, in himself, a fire temple. He must seek to unite the fire within him to the flame of divine righteousness.

Abbreviations used in the text

AHM: I. Gershevitch, *The Avestan Hymn to Mithra*. See Bibliography.

AV: *Ardā Virāf Nāmag*, translated by Haug. See Bibliography

Boyce, Sources: Boyce, *Sources for the study of Zoroastrianism*. See Bibliography.

BTA: B. T. Anklesaria, *Zand-Akāsīh*. See Bibliography.

Boyd, J., and Kotwal, F. 'The Zoroastrian paragṇā, *Journal of Mithraic Studies*, II, 1977, pp. 18–52.

Contra Celsum, E. T. by H. Chadwick, Cambridge, 1965.

De antro Nympharum. The Cave of the Nymphs in the Odyssey, ed. and trans. Seminar Classics 609, State University of New York at Buffalo, 1969.

D-G, Hymns: Duchesne-Guillemin, *The Hymns of Zarathustra*. See Bibliography.

D-G, Symbols: Duchesne-Guillemin, *Symbols and Values in Zoroastrianism*. See Bibliography.

Dhalla, Nyaishes: Dhalla, *The Nyaishes or Zoroastrian Litanies*. See Bibliography.

D.i.D: *Dādistān ī Dēnīk*, a Pahlavi text.

Dk: *Dēnkard*, a Pahlavi text.

Dk.M: Madan's edition of the *Dēnkard*.

G.Bd: The Greater or Iranian edition of the *Bundahishn*, a Pahlavi text.

Gershevitch: I. Gershevitch's article 'Iranian Literature'. See Bibliography.

Gray, Foundations: Gray, *The Foundations of the Iranian Religions*. See Bibliography.

Kent, R. G.: Kent, *Old Persian Grammar, Texts, Lexicon*, New Haven, 1953.

Levy: Levy, *The Epic of the Kings*. See Bibliography.

MB. Pious Foundations: M. Boyce, 'The Pious Foundations of the Zoroastrians', *Bulletin of the School of Oriental and African Studies*, 31, 1968.

MEZ: Moulton, *Early Zoroastrianism*. See Bibliography.

M.Kh: *Mēnōg-i Khrad*, a Pahlavi text.

Modi, R. C.: Modi, *The Religious Ceremonies and Customs of the Parsees*. See Bibliography.

Modi, Cat: Modi, *Catechism of the Zoroastrian Religion*. See Bibliography.

MWS: Smith, Translation of the *Gāthās*. See Bibliography.

Noss, J. B.: Noss, *Man's Religions*, New York, 1968.

RV: *Rig-Veda*, an ancient Indian text.

S.B: *Shatapatha-Brahmana*, an ancient Indian text.

Shaked, Notes: S. Shaked, 'Some Notes on Ahreman, The Evil Spirit, and his Creation', in *Studies in Mysticism and Religion*, Studies in honour of G. Scholem, Jerusalem, 1967.

Wolff, *Das Avesta*. See Bibliography.

Ys: *Yasna* (Part of the Zoroastrian bible, the Avesta).

Yt: *Yasht* (Part of the Zoroastrian bible, the Avesta).

ZDT: Zaehner, *Dawn and Twilight of Zoroastrianism*. See Bibliography.

ZS. MB. R: *Zādspram*, the particular text used in this book is translated by M. Boyce in 'Rapithwin. No Ruz and the Feast of Sade', in *Pratidanam*, studies in honour of F. B. K. Kuiper, The Hague, 1968.

ZT: Zaehner, *Teachings of the Magi*. See Bibliography.

Acknowledgments

A. C. L., Brussels 53; Aerofilms, Boreham Wood 6–7; Archaeological Museum, Istanbul 69; Professor Sir Harold Bailey, Cambridge 70, 118 top, 118 bottom, 119 top, 119 bottom; Bibliothèque Nationale, Paris 115, 117; Dr A. D. H. Bivar, London 13 top left, 13 bottom right, 39 top right, 39 bottom right; Bodleian Library, Oxford 57; Professor Mary Boyce, London 61, 62, 64 top, 135, 137 top left, 137 bottom left, 137 right; British Museum, London frontispiece, 26, 27, 100, 108; R. M. D. Chamarbangrala, RMDC Press, Bombay 94 left, 94 right; C. M. Daniels, Newcastle upon Tyne 13 left, 84 top, 84 bottom, 84–5 top, 84–5 bottom, 85 top, 85 centre, 85 bottom, 88 bottom; John Dayton, London 103; John Donat, London half-title page, 93; Professor Dr F. K. Dörner, Nürnberg 24, 28 left, 28 right, 29; Freer Gallery of Art, Washington, DC 17; Photographie Giraudon, Paris 111; Georgina Herrmann, Market Harborough 14 bottom, 42–3, 46–7, 50–51, 58, 99, 106, 107 top; Hermitage Museum, Leningrad 41 left; Dr. B. Heükemes, Kupfälzisches Museum, Heidelberg 88–9; Professor John Hinnells, Manchester 14 top left, 14 top right, 19 top, 32 left, 32 right, 45, 59, 63, 66–67, 67, 75, 76, 78, 78–9, 80, 81 top, 82–83, 83, 86–87, 88 top, 88 centre, 90 top, 90 bottom, 95, 96, 102 bottom, 105, 121, 122, 123 top, 123 bottom, 124, 128 left, 128 centre, 128 right, 129 left, 129 centre, 129 right, 130–131, 131, 132 top left, 132 top right, 132 centre, 133 left, 136; Mark Hinnells, Manchester 126 left, 126 right, 126 bottom right, 127 top, 127 bottom left, 127 bottom right, 139; Holle Verlag, Baden-Baden 15, 107 bottom, 109; Kölnisches Stadtmuseum 80; Foto Kral, Hainburg 81 bottom; The Metropolitan Museum of Art, New York 36–37, 40, 114; Museum of Antiquities of the University of Newcastle upon Tyne, 88 bottom; The Museum of London 91; Newnes Books, Feltham 30, 35, 41 right, 45 top right, 45 bottom right, 48 top, 48 bottom, 49 top, 49 bottom, 64 bottom, 72–73 top, 72–73 bottom, 104, 112–113; The Open University, Milton Keynes 77 (based on figure 2 from Units 26–28 AD208 *Man's Religious Quest*); Penguin Books Limited 22 (Fig. 4.3, drawn by Raymond Turvey, from *A Handbook of Living Religions*, ed. John R. Hinnells, Viking Penguin Inc., 1984, p. 177, copyright © John R. Hinnells and Penguin Books Ltd., 1984. Used by permission); Antonello Perissinotto, Padua 8, 9, 10 top, 11, 100–101, 116; Photoresources, Canterbury 19 bottom; Popperfoto, London 97; Josephine Powell, Rome 18, 23 left, 23 right, 25, 38, 102 top; Roger-Viollet, Paris 12; Staatliche Museen Preussischer Kulturbesitz, Berlin 399, left; Weidenfeld and Nicolson, London 31; Roger Wood, London 10 bottom, 54–55.

The author wishes to express his thanks to the various museums where he has been permitted to photograph Mithraic objects.

Every effort has been made to contact museums where photographs have been taken. The publishers would be glad to hear from any source not fully acknowledged.

The author wishes to express his profound thanks to Miss Nora Firby for her work on the Index and proofs.

The author wishes to express his gratitude to Professor R. Beck of Erindale College, Toronto University, for permission to study and use some of his publications still in press, and for his help with the redrafting of the chapter on Mithraism.

Further Reading List

Books in English

Anklesaria, B. T. *Zand Ākāsīh*, Bombay, 1956.
—— *Zand-ī Vohūman Yasn*, Bombay, 1957.
Bianchi, U., *Mysteria Mithrae*, Leiden, 1979.
Boyce, M., *A History of Zoroastrian*, Brill, 2 vols., 1975 and 1982.
—— *A Persian Stronghold of Zoroastrianism*, Oxford, 1977.
—— *Zoroastrians: their religious beliefs and practices*, London, 1979.
—— *Textual Sources for the Study of Zoroastrianism*, Manchester, 1984.
Cameron, C. G., *History of Early Iran*, Chicago, 1936.
Carnoy, A. J., 'Iranian Mythology' in *Mythology of all Races*, Vol. VI, ed. L. H. Gray, New York, 1964.
Cumont, F., *The Mysteries of Mithra*, New York, 1956.
Dhalla, M. N., *The Nyaishes or Zoroastrian Litanies*, New York, 1965.
Duchesne-Guillemin, J., *The Hymns of Zarathustra*, London, 1952.
—— *The Western Response to Zoroaster*, Oxford, 1958.
—— *Symbols and Values in Zoroastrianism*, New York, 1966.
—— *Études Mithriaques*, Leiden, 1978.
Frye, R. N., *The Heritage of Persia*, 2nd edn., London, 1976.
Gershevitch, I., 'Iranian Literature' in *Literatures of the East*, ed. E. B. Ceadel, London, 1953.
—— *The Avestan Hymn to Mithra*, Cambridge, 1959.
Ghirshman, R., *Iran*, London, 1961.
—— *Persia from the Origins to Alexander the Great*, London, 1964.
—— *Iran, Parthians and Sasanians*, London, 1962.
Gray, L. H., *The Foundations of the Iranian Religions*, Bombay, 1925.
Haug, M., and West, E. W., *The Book of Ardā Virāf*. Bombay-London, 1872–4.

Herrmann, G., *The Iranian Revival*, Oxford, 1977.
Hinnells, J. R., *Mithraic Studies*, Manchester, 1975.
—— *Zoroastrianism and the Parsis*, London, 1981
Insler, S., *The Gāthās of Zarathushtra*, Leiden, 1975.
Jackson, A. V. W., *Zoroaster, The Prophet of Ancient Iran*, New York, 1965.
—— *Zoroastrian Studies*, New York, 1965.
Kulke, E., *The Parsees in India*, Munich, 1974.
Levy, R., *The Epic of the Kings, Shāh-nāma*, London, 1967.
Modi, J. J. *The Religious Ceremonies and Customs of the Parsees*, Bombay, 1937.
—— *A Catechism of the Zoroastrian Religion*, Bombay, 1962.
Moulton, J. H. *Early Zoroastrianism*, London, 1913.
Pavry, J. D. C., *The Zoroastrian Doctrine of a Future Life*, New York, 1965.
Pope, A. E., and Ackerman, P. (eds.), *A Survey of Persian Art*, Vols. I–IV, Oxford, 1938.
Porada, E., *Ancient Iran, The Art of Pre-Islamic Times*, London, 1965.
Sacred Books of the East, Vols 4, 5, 18, 23, 24, 31, 37, 47 contain translations of a number of Zoroastrian texts, some of which remain the only English translation available.
Schmidt, E. F., *Persepolis I–III*, Chicago, 1953, 1957, 1971.
Shaked, S., *Wisdom of the Sasanian Sages*, Boulder, Colorado, 1979.
Smith, M. W., *Studies in the Syntax of the Gathas of Zarathushtra Together with Text Translation, and Notes*, New York, 1966.
Spuler, B., *Iranistik Literatur* in *Handbuch der Orientalistik*, IV, 2, 1, Leiden, 1968.
Stronach, D., *Pasargadae*, Oxford, 1978.
Thieme, P., *Mithra Aryaman*, New Haven, 1958.
Vermaseren, M. J., *Mithras, The Sacred God*,

London, 1963.
—— *Corpus Inscriptionum et Monumentorum Religionis Mithriacae*, The Hague, 1956, 1960.
Yarshater, E. (ed.), *Cambridge History of Iran*, Vol. 3 (2 parts), Seleucid, Parthian and Sasanian periods, Cambridge, 1983.
Zaehner, R. C., *Zurvan, A Zoroastrian Dilemma*, Oxford, 1955.
—— *The Teachings of the Magi*, London, 1966.
—— *The Dawn and Twilight of Zoroastrianism*, London, 1961.

Books in French

Christiansen, A., *Les Types du premier Homme et du roi*, Stockholm-Leiden, 1917–1934.
Cumont, F., *Textes Monuments figurés relatifs aux mystères de Mithra*, I–II, Brussels, 1896–9.
Duchesne-Guillemin, *La Religion de L'Iran Ancien*, Paris, 1962, (E. T. by K. M. JamaspAsa, Bombay, 1973).
Menasce, J. de, *Le Troisième Livre du Dēnkart*, Paris, 1977.
Mole, M., *Culte, Mythe et Cosmologie dans L'Iran Ancien*, Paris, 1963.
—— *La legende de Zoroastre selon les textes Pahlavis*, Paris, 1967.
Varenne, J., *Zarathushtra et la tradition Mazdéenne*, Paris, 1966.

Books in German

Humbach, H., *Die Gathas des Zarathustra*, Heidelberg, 1959.
Lommel, H., *Die Väst's des Awesta*, Göttingen, 1927.
—— *Die Religion Zarathushtras*, Tübingen, 1930.
Widengren, G., *Die Religionen Irans*, Stuttgart, 1965.
Wolff, F., *Das Avesta Die Heiligen Bücher der Parsen*, Strassburg, Berlin, reprinted 1960.

Index